Elastic Load Balancing Classic Load Balancers

A catalogue record for this book is available from the Hong Kong Public Libraries.

Published in Hong Kong by Samurai Media Limited.

Email: info@samuraimedia.org

ISBN 9789888408269

Contents

What Is a Classic Load Balancer?

Elastic Load Balancing supports three types of load balancers: Application Load Balancers, Network Load Balancers, and Classic Load Balancers. This guide discusses Classic Load Balancers. For more information about Application Load Balancers, see the User Guide for Application Load Balancers. For more information about Network Load Balancers, see the User Guide for Network Load Balancers.

Classic Load Balancer Overview

A load balancer distributes incoming application traffic across multiple EC2 instances in multiple Availability Zones. This increases the fault tolerance of your applications. Elastic Load Balancing detects unhealthy instances and routes traffic only to healthy instances.

Your load balancer serves as a single point of contact for clients. This increases the availability of your application. You can add and remove instances from your load balancer as your needs change, without disrupting the overall flow of requests to your application. Elastic Load Balancing scales your load balancer as traffic to your application changes over time. Elastic Load Balancing can scale to the vast majority of workloads automatically.

A *listener* checks for connection requests from clients, using the protocol and port that you configure, and forwards requests to one or more registered instances using the protocol and port number that you configure. You add one or more listeners to your load balancer.

You can configure *health checks*, which are used to monitor the health of the registered instances so that the load balancer only sends requests to the healthy instances.

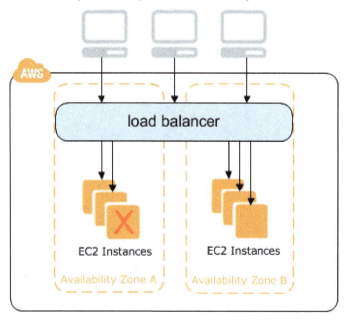

To ensure that your registered instances are able to handle the request load in each Availability Zone, it is important to keep approximately the same number of instances in each Availability Zone registered with the load balancer. For example, if you have ten instances in Availability Zone us-west-2a and two instances in us-west-2b, the requests are distributed evenly between the two Availability Zones. As a result, the two instances in us-west-2b serve the same amount of traffic as the ten instances in us-west-2a. Instead, you should have six instances in each Availability Zone.

By default, the load balancer distributes traffic evenly across the Availability Zones that you enable for your load balancer. To distribute traffic evenly across all registered instances in all enabled Availability Zones, enable *cross-zone load balancing* on your load balancer. However, we still recommend that you maintain approximately equivalent numbers of instances in each Availability Zone for better fault tolerance.

For more information, see How Elastic Load Balancing Works in the *Elastic Load Balancing User Guide*.

Benefits

Using a Classic Load Balancer instead of an Application Load Balancer has the following benefits:

- Support for EC2-Classic
- Support for TCP and SSL listeners
- Support for sticky sessions using application-generated cookies

For more information about the features supported by each load balancer type, see Comparison of Elastic Load Balancing Products.

How to Get Started

- To learn how to create a Classic Load Balancer and register EC2 instances with it, see Tutorial: Create a Classic Load Balancer.
- To learn how to create an HTTPS load balancer and register EC2 instances with it, see Create a Classic Load Balancer with an HTTPS Listener.
- To learn how to use the various features supported by Elastic Load Balancing, see Configure Your Classic Load Balancer.

Pricing

With your load balancer, you pay only for what you use. For more information, see Elastic Load Balancing Pricing.

Tutorial: Create a Classic Load Balancer

This tutorial provides a hands-on introduction to Classic Load Balancers through the AWS Management Console, a web-based interface. You'll create a load balancer that receives public HTTP traffic and sends it to your EC2 instances.

Note that you can create your load balancer for use with EC2-Classic or a VPC. Some of the tasks described in this tutorial apply only to load balancers in a VPC.

Topics

- Before You Begin
- Step 1: Select a Load Balancer Type
- Step 2: Define Your Load Balancer
- Step 3: Assign Security Groups to Your Load Balancer in a VPC
- Step 4: Configure Health Checks for Your EC2 Instances
- Step 5: Register EC2 Instances with Your Load Balancer
- Step 6: Tag Your Load Balancer (Optional)
- Step 7: Create and Verify Your Load Balancer
- Step 8: Delete Your Load Balancer (Optional)

Before You Begin

- Complete the steps in Prepare Your VPC and EC2 Instances.
- Launch the EC2 instances that you plan to register with your load balancer. Ensure that the security groups for these instances allow HTTP access on port 80.
- Install a web server, such as Apache or Internet Information Services (IIS), on each instance, enter its DNS name into the address field of an Internet-connected web browser, and verify that the browser displays the default page of the server.

Step 1: Select a Load Balancer Type

Elastic Load Balancing supports three types of load balancers: Application Load Balancers, Network Load Balancers, and Classic Load Balancers. For this tutorial, you create a Classic Load Balancer. Alternatively, to create an Application Load Balancer, see Getting Started with Application Load Balancers in the *User Guide for Application Load Balancers*. To create a Network Load Balancer, see Getting Started with Network Load Balancers in the *User Guide for Network Load Balancers*.

To create a Classic Load Balancer

1. Open the Amazon EC2 console at https://console.aws.amazon.com/ec2/.

2. On the navigation bar, choose a region for your load balancer. Be sure to select the same region that you selected for your EC2 instances.

3. On the navigation pane, under **LOAD BALANCING**, choose **Load Balancers**.

4. Choose **Create Load Balancer**.

5. For **Classic Load Balancer**, choose **Create**.

Step 2: Define Your Load Balancer

You must provide a basic configuration for your load balancer, such as a name, a network, and a listener.

A *listener* is a process that checks for connection requests. It is configured with a protocol and a port for front-end (client to load balancer) connections and a protocol and a port for back-end (load balancer to instance) connections. In this tutorial, you configure a listener that accepts HTTP requests on port 80 and sends them to your instances on port 80 using HTTP.

To define your load balancer and listener

1. For **Load Balancer name**, type a name for your load balancer.

   The name of your Classic Load Balancer must be unique within your set of Classic Load Balancers for the region, can have a maximum of 32 characters, can contain only alphanumeric characters and hyphens, and must not begin or end with a hyphen.

2. For **Create LB inside**, select the same network that you selected for your instances: EC2-Classic or a specific VPC.

3. [Default VPC] If you selected a default VPC and would like to choose the subnets for your load balancer, select **Enable advanced VPC configuration**.

4. Leave the default listener configuration.

5. [EC2-VPC] For **Available subnets**, select at least one available public subnet using its add icon. The subnet is moved under **Selected subnets**. To improve the availability of your load balancer, select more than one public subnet. **Note**
   If you selected EC2-Classic as your network, or you have a default VPC but did not select **Enable advanced VPC configuration**, you do not see the user interface to select subnets.

   You can add at most one subnet per Availability Zone. If you select a subnet from an Availability Zone where there is already an selected subnet, this subnet replaces the currently selected subnet for the Availability Zone.

Available subnets

Actions	Availability Zone	Subnet ID	Subnet CIDR	Name
⊕	us-west-2c	subnet-cb663da2	10.0.1.0/24	
⊕	us-west-2c	subnet-c9663da0	10.0.0.0/24	

Selected subnets

Actions	Availability Zone	Subnet ID	Subnet CIDR	Name
⊖	us-west-2a	subnet-e4f33493	10.0.2.0/24	
⊖	us-west-2b	subnet-5264e837	10.0.3.0/24	

6. Choose **Next: Assign Security Groups**.

Step 3: Assign Security Groups to Your Load Balancer in a VPC

If you selected a VPC as your network, you must assign your load balancer a security group that allows inbound traffic to the ports that you specified for your load balancer and the health checks for your load balancer.

Note
If you selected EC2-Classic as your network, you can continue to the next step. By default, Elastic Load Balancing provides a security group for load balancers in EC2-Classic.

To assign security group to your load balancer

1. On the **Assign Security Groups** page, select **Create a new security group**.

2. Type a name and description for your security group, or leave the default name and description. This new security group contains a rule that allows traffic to the port that you configured your load balancer to use.

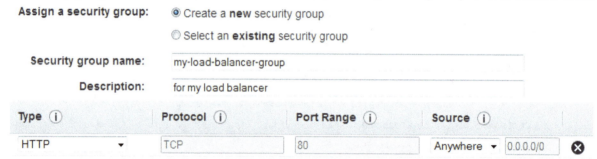

3. Choose **Next: Configure Security Settings**.

4. For this tutorial, you are not using a secure listener. Choose **Next: Configure Health Check** to continue to the next step.

Step 4: Configure Health Checks for Your EC2 Instances

Elastic Load Balancing automatically checks the health of the EC2 instances for your load balancer. If Elastic Load Balancing finds an unhealthy instance, it stops sending traffic to the instance and reroutes traffic to healthy instances. In this step, you customize the health checks for your load balancer.

To configure health checks for your instances

1. On the **Configure Health Check** page, leave **Ping Protocol** set to HTTP and **Ping Port** set to 80.

2. For **Ping Path**, replace the default value with a single forward slash ("/"). This tells Elastic Load Balancing to send health check queries to the default home page for your web server, such as `index.html`.

3. For **Advanced Details**, leave the default values.

4. Choose **Next: Add EC2 Instances**.

Step 5: Register EC2 Instances with Your Load Balancer

Your load balancer distributes traffic between the instances that are registered to it.

Note
When you register an instance with an elastic network interface (ENI) attached, the load balancer routes traffic to the primary IP address of the primary interface (eth0) of the instance.

To register EC2 instances with your load balancer

1. On the **Add EC2 Instances** page, select the instances to register with your load balancer.

2. Leave cross-zone load balancing and connection draining enabled.

3. Choose **Next: Add Tags**.

Alternatively, you can register instances with your load balancer later on using the following options:

- Select running instances after you create the load balancer. For more information, see Register Instances with Your Load Balancer.
- Set up Auto Scaling to register the instances automatically when it launches them. For more information, see Set Up a Scaled and Load-Balanced Application in the *Amazon EC2 Auto Scaling User Guide*.

Step 6: Tag Your Load Balancer (Optional)

You can tag your load balancer, or continue to the next step. Note that you can tag your load balancer later on; for more information, see Tag Your Classic Load Balancer.

To add tags to your load balancer

1. On the **Add Tags** page, specify a key and a value for the tag.

2. To add another tag, choose **Create Tag** and specify a key and a value for the tag.

3. After you are finished adding tags, choose **Review and Create**.

Step 7: Create and Verify Your Load Balancer

Before you create the load balancer, review the settings that you selected. After creating the load balancer, you can verify that it's sending traffic to your EC2 instances.

To create and test your load balancer

1. On the **Review** page, choose **Create**.

2. After you are notified that your load balancer was created, choose **Close**.

3. Select your new load balancer.

4. On the **Description** tab, check the **Status** row. If it indicates that some of your instances are not in service, its probably because they are still in the registration process. For more information, see Troubleshoot a Classic Load Balancer: Instance Registration.

5. After at least one of your EC2 instances is in service, you can test your load balancer. Copy the string from **DNS name** (for example, my-load-balancer-1234567890.us-west-2.elb.amazonaws.com) and paste it into the address field of an Internet-connected web browser. If your load balancer is working, you see the default page of your server.

Step 8: Delete Your Load Balancer (Optional)

As soon as your load balancer becomes available, you are billed for each hour or partial hour that you keep it running. When you no longer need a load balancer, you can delete it. As soon as the load balancer is deleted, you stop incurring charges for it. Note that deleting a load balancer does not affect the instances registered with the load balancer.

To delete your load balancer

1. If you have a CNAME record for your domain that points to your load balancer, point it to a new location and wait for the DNS change to take effect before deleting your load balancer.

2. Open the Amazon EC2 console at https://console.aws.amazon.com/ec2/.

3. On the navigation pane, under **LOAD BALANCING**, choose **Load Balancers**.

4. Select the load balancer.

5. Choose **Actions, Delete**.

6. When prompted for confirmation, choose **Yes, Delete**.

7. (Optional) After you delete a load balancer, the EC2 instances associated with the load balancer continue to run, and you are billed for each hour or partial hour that you keep them running. For information about stopping or terminating your instances, see Stop and Start Your Instance or Terminate Your Instance in the *Amazon EC2 User Guide for Linux Instances*.

Internet-Facing Classic Load Balancers

An Internet-facing load balancer has a publicly resolvable DNS name, so it can route requests from clients over the Internet to the EC2 instances that are registered with the load balancer.

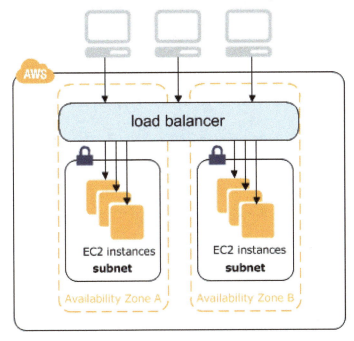

If a load balancer is in a VPC with ClassicLink enabled, its instances can be linked EC2-Classic instances. If a load balancer is in EC2-Classic, its instances must be in EC2-Classic.

Topics

- Public DNS Names for Your Load Balancer
- Create an Internet-Facing Load Balancer

Public DNS Names for Your Load Balancer

When your load balancer is created, it receives a public DNS name that clients can use to send requests. The DNS servers resolve the DNS name of your load balancer to the public IP addresses of the load balancer nodes for your load balancer. Each load balancer node is connected to the back-end instances using private IP addresses.

EC2-VPC

Load balancers in a VPC support IPv4 addresses only. The console displays a public DNS name with the following form:

```
1 name-1234567890.region.elb.amazonaws.com
```

EC2-Classic

Load balancers in EC2-Classic support both IPv4 and IPv6 addresses. The console displays the following public DNS names:

```
1 name-123456789.region.elb.amazonaws.com
2 ipv6.name-123456789.region.elb.amazonaws.com
3 dualstack.name-123456789.region.elb.amazonaws.com
```

The base public DNS name returns only IPv4 records. The public DNS name with the `ipv6` prefix returns only IPv6 records. The public DNS name with the `dualstack` prefix returns both IPv4 and IPv6 records. We recommend that you enable IPv6 support by using the DNS name with the `dualstack` prefix to ensure that clients can access the load balancer using either IPv4 or IPv6.

Clients can connect to your load balancer in EC2-Classic using either IPv4 or IPv6. However, communication between the load balancer and its back-end instances uses only IPv4, regardless of how the client communicates with your load balancer.

Create an Internet-Facing Load Balancer

When you create a load balancer in a VPC, you can make it an internal load balancer or an Internet-facing load balancer. You create an Internet-facing load balancer in a public subnet. Load balancers in EC2-Classic are always Internet-facing load balancers.

When you create your load balancer, you configure listeners, configure health checks, and register back-end instances. You configure a listener by specifying a protocol and a port for front-end (client to load balancer) connections, and a protocol and a port for back-end (load balancer to back-end instances) connections. You can configure multiple listeners for your load balancer.

To create a basic Internet-facing load balancer, see Tutorial: Create a Classic Load Balancer.

To create a load balancer with an HTTPS listener, see Create a Classic Load Balancer with an HTTPS Listener.

Internal Classic Load Balancers

When you create a load balancer in a VPC, you must choose whether to make it an internal load balancer or an Internet-facing load balancer.

The nodes of an Internet-facing load balancer have public IP addresses. The DNS name of an Internet-facing load balancer is publicly resolvable to the public IP addresses of the nodes. Therefore, Internet-facing load balancers can route requests from clients over the Internet. For more information, see Internet-Facing Classic Load Balancers.

The nodes of an internal load balancer have only private IP addresses. The DNS name of an internal load balancer is publicly resolvable to the private IP addresses of the nodes. Therefore, internal load balancers can only route requests from clients with access to the VPC for the load balancer.

If your application has multiple tiers, for example web servers that must be connected to the Internet and database servers that are only connected to the web servers, you can design an architecture that uses both internal and Internet-facing load balancers. Create an Internet-facing load balancer and register the web servers with it. Create an internal load balancer and register the database servers with it. The web servers receive requests from the Internet-facing load balancer and send requests for the database servers to the internal load balancer. The database servers receive requests from the internal load balancer.

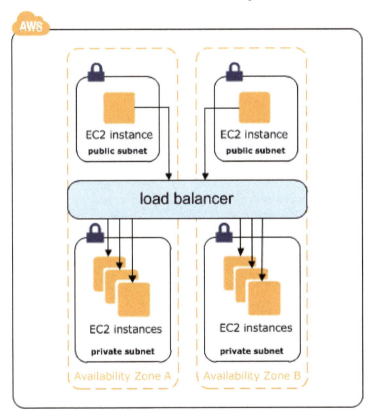

Topics

- Public DNS Name for Your Load Balancer
- Create an Internal Classic Load Balancer

Public DNS Name for Your Load Balancer

When an internal load balancer is created, it receives a public DNS name with the following form:

```
1  internal-name-123456789.region.elb.amazonaws.com
```

The DNS servers resolve the DNS name of your load balancer to the private IP addresses of the load balancer nodes for your internal load balancer. Each load balancer node is connected to the private IP addresses of the back-end instances using elastic network interfaces. If cross-zone load balancing is enabled, each node is connected to each back-end instance, regardless of Availability Zone. Otherwise, each node is connected only to the instances that are in its Availability Zone.

Create an Internal Classic Load Balancer

You can create an internal load balancer to distribute traffic to your EC2 instances from clients with access to the VPC for the load balancer.

Topics

- Prerequisites
- Create an Internal Load Balancer Using the Console
- Create an Internal Load Balancer Using the AWS CLI

Prerequisites

- If you have not yet created a VPC for your load balancer, you must create it before you get started. For more information, see Prepare Your VPC and EC2 Instances.
- Launch the EC2 instances that you plan to register with your internal load balancer. Ensure that you launch them in private subnets in the VPC intended for the load balancer.

Create an Internal Load Balancer Using the Console

By default, Elastic Load Balancing creates an Internet-facing load balancer. Use the following procedure to create an internal load balancer and register your EC2 instances with the newly created internal load balancer.

To create an internal load balancer

1. Open the Amazon EC2 console at https://console.aws.amazon.com/ec2/.

2. On the navigation pane, under **LOAD BALANCING**, choose **Load Balancers**.

3. Choose **Create Load Balancer**.

4. For **Select load balancer type**, choose **Classic Load Balancer**.

5. On the **Define Load Balancer** page, do the following:

   1. For **Load Balancer name**, type a name for your load balancer.

      The name of your Classic Load Balancer must be unique within your set of Classic Load Balancers for the region, can have a maximum of 32 characters, can contain only alphanumeric characters and hyphens, and must not begin or end with a hyphen.

   2. For **Create LB inside**, select a VPC for your load balancer.

   3. Choose **Create an internal load balancer**.

   4. [Default VPC] If you selected a default VPC and would like to select subnets for your load balancer, choose **Enable advanced VPC configuration**.

   5. Leave the default listener configuration.

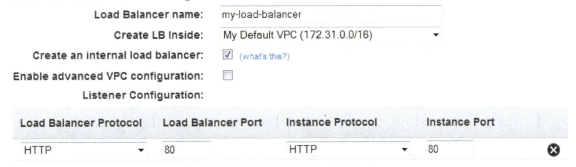

6. For **Available subnets**, select at least one available subnet using its add icon. The subnet is moved under **Selected subnets**. To improve the availability of your load balancer, select more than one subnet. **Note**
If you selected a default VPC as your network, but did not select **Enable advanced VPC configuration**, you do not have the option to select subnets.

You can attach at most one subnet per Availability Zone. If you select a subnet from an Availability Zone where there is already an attached subnet, this subnet replaces the currently attached subnet for the Availability Zone.

7. Choose **Next: Assign Security Groups**.

6. On the **Assign Security Groups** page, choose **Create a new security group**. Enter a name and description for your security group, or leave the default name and description. This new security group contains a rule that allows traffic to the port that you configured your load balancer to use. If you will use a different port for the health checks, you must choose **Add Rule** to add a rule that allows inbound traffic to that port as well. Choose **Next: Configure Security Settings**.

7. On the **Configure Security Settings** page, choose **Next: Configure Health Check** to continue to the next step. If you prefer to create a HTTPS load balancer, see HTTPS Listeners for Your Classic Load Balancer.

8. On the **Configure Health Check** page, configure the health check settings that your application requires, and then choose **Next: Add EC2 Instances**.

9. On the **Add EC2 Instances** page, select the instances to register with your load balancer, and then choose **Next: Add Tags**. **Note**
When you register an instance with an elastic network interface (ENI) attached, the load balancer routes traffic to the primary IP address of the primary interface (eth0) of the instance.

10. (Optional) You can add tags to your load balancer. When you are finished adding tags, choose **Review and Create**.

11. On the **Review** page, check your settings. If you need to make changes, choose the corresponding link to edit the settings. When you are finished, choose **Create**.

12. After you are notified that your load balancer was created, choose **Close**.

13. Select your new load balancer.

14. On the **Description** tab, note that **DNS name** and **Scheme** indicate that the load balancer is internal.

Check the **Status** row. If it indicates that some of your instances are not in service, its probably because they are still in the registration process. For more information, see Troubleshoot a Classic Load Balancer: Instance Registration.

Create an Internal Load Balancer Using the AWS CLI

By default, Elastic Load Balancing creates an Internet-facing load balancer. Use the following procedure to create an internal load balancer and register your EC2 instances with the newly created internal load balancer.

To create an internal load balancer

1. Use the create-load-balancer command with the --scheme option set to internal, as follows:

```
1 aws elb create-load-balancer --load-balancer-name my-internal-loadbalancer --listeners
    Protocol=HTTP,LoadBalancerPort=80,InstanceProtocol=HTTP,InstancePort=80
2 --subnets subnet-4e05f721 --scheme internal --security-groups sg-b9ffedd5
```

The following is an example response. Note that the name indicates that this is an internal load balancer.

```
1 {
2     "DNSName": "internal-my-internal-loadbalancer-786501203.us-west-2.elb.amazonaws.com"
3 }
```

2. Use the following register-instances-with-load-balancer command to add instances:

```
1 aws elb register-instances-with-load-balancer --load-balancer-name my-internal-loadbalancer
     --instances i-4f8cf126 i-0bb7ca62
```

The following is an example response:

```
1 {
2     "Instances": [
3         {
4             "InstanceId": "i-4f8cf126"
5         },
6         {
7             "InstanceId": "i-0bb7ca62"
8         }
9     ]
10 }
```

3. (Optional) Use the following describe-load-balancers command to verify the internal load balancer:

```
1 aws elb describe-load-balancers --load-balancer-name my-internal-loadbalancer
```

The response includes the DNSName and Scheme fields, which indicate that this is an internal load balancer.

```
1 {
2     "LoadBalancerDescriptions": [
3         {
4             ...
5             "DNSName": "internal-my-internal-loadbalancer-1234567890.us-west-2.elb.
                 amazonaws.com",
6             "SecurityGroups": [
7                 "sg-b9ffedd5"
8             ],
9             "Policies": {
10                 "LBCookieStickinessPolicies": [],
11                 "AppCookieStickinessPolicies": [],
12                 "OtherPolicies": []
13             },
14             "LoadBalancerName": "my-internal-loadbalancer",
15             "CreatedTime": "2014-05-22T20:32:19.920Z",
16             "AvailabilityZones": [
17                 "us-west-2a"
18             ],
19             "Scheme": "internal",
20             ...
21         }
22     ]
23 }
```

Registered Instances for Your Classic Load Balancer

After you've created your Classic Load Balancer, you must register your EC2 instances with the load balancer. You can select EC2 instances from a single Availability Zone or multiple Availability Zones within the same region as the load balancer. Elastic Load Balancing routinely performs health checks on registered EC2 instances, and automatically distributes incoming requests to the DNS name of your load balancer across the registered, healthy EC2 instances.

Topics

- Best Practices for Your Instances
- Prepare Your VPC and EC2 Instances
- Configure Health Checks for Your Classic Load Balancer
- Configure Security Groups for Your Classic Load Balancer
- Add or Remove Availability Zones for Your Load Balancer in EC2-Classic
- Add or Remove Subnets for Your Classic Load Balancer in a VPC
- Register or Deregister EC2 Instances for Your Classic Load Balancer

Best Practices for Your Instances

- Install a web server, such as Apache or Internet Information Services (IIS), on all instances that you plan to register with your load balancer.
- For HTTP and HTTPS listeners, we recommend that you enable the keep-alive option in your EC2 instances, which enables the load balancer to re-use the connections to your instances for multiple client requests. This reduces the load on your web server and improves the throughput of the load balancer. The keep-alive timeout should be at least 60 seconds to ensure that the load balancer is responsible for closing the connection to your instance.
- Elastic Load Balancing supports Path Maximum Transmission Unit (MTU) Discovery. To ensure that Path MTU Discovery can function correctly, you must ensure that the security group for your instance allows ICMP fragmentation required (type 3, code 4) messages. For more information, see Path MTU Discovery in the *Amazon EC2 User Guide for Linux Instances*.

Prepare Your VPC and EC2 Instances

We recommend that you launch your instances and create your load balancer in a virtual private cloud (VPC). If you have a new AWS account or plan to use a region that you haven't used before, you have a default VPC. You can use a default VPC if you have one, or create your own VPC.

Load Balancers in a VPC

Amazon Virtual Private Cloud (Amazon VPC) enables you to define a virtual networking environment in a private, isolated section of the AWS cloud. Within this virtual private cloud (VPC), you can launch AWS resources such as load balancers and EC2 instances. For more information, see the *Amazon VPC User Guide*.

Subnets for Your Load Balancer

To ensure that your load balancer can scale properly, verify that each subnet for your load balancer has a CIDR block with at least a /27 bitmask (for example, 10.0.0.0/27) and has at least 8 free IP addresses. Your load balancer uses these IP addresses to establish connections with the instances.

Create a subnet in each Availability Zone where you want to launch instances. Depending on your application, you can launch your instances in public subnets, private subnets, or a combination of public and private subnets. A public subnet has a route to an Internet gateway. Note that default VPCs have one public subnet per Availability Zone by default.

When you create a load balancer, you must add one or more public subnets to the load balancer. If your instances are in private subnets, create public subnets in the same Availability Zones as the subnets with your instances;

22

you will add these public subnets to the load balancer.

Security Groups

You must ensure that the load balancer can communicate with your instances on both the listener port and the health check port. For more information, see Security Groups for Load Balancers in a VPC. The security group for your instances must allow traffic in both directions on both ports for each subnet for your load balancer. For more information, see Security Groups for Instances in a VPC.

Network ACLs

The network ACLs for your VPC must allow traffic in both directions on the listener port and the health check port. For more information, see Network ACLs for Load Balancers in a VPC.

ClassicLink

ClassicLink enables your EC2-Classic instances to communicate with VPC instances using private IP addresses, provided that the VPC security groups allow it. If you plan to register linked EC2-Classic instances with your load balancer, you must enable ClassicLink for your VPC, and then create your load balancer in the ClassicLink-enabled VPC. For more information, see ClassicLink Basics and Working with ClassicLink in the *Amazon EC2 User Guide for Linux Instances.*

Configure Health Checks for Your Classic Load Balancer

To discover the availability of your EC2 instances, a load balancer periodically sends pings, attempts connections, or sends requests to test the EC2 instances. These tests are called *health checks*. The status of the instances that are healthy at the time of the health check is `InService`. The status of any instances that are unhealthy at the time of the health check is `OutOfService`. The load balancer performs health checks on all registered instances, whether the instance is in a healthy state or an unhealthy state.

The load balancer routes requests only to the healthy instances. When the load balancer determines that an instance is unhealthy, it stops routing requests to that instance. The load balancer resumes routing requests to the instance when it has been restored to a healthy state.

The load balancer checks the health of the registered instances using either the default health check configuration provided by Elastic Load Balancing or a health check configuration that you configure.

If you have associated your Auto Scaling group with a Classic load balancer, you can use the load balancer health check to determine the health state of instances in your Auto Scaling group. By default, an Auto Scaling group periodically determines the health state of each instance. For more information, see Add an Elastic Load Balancing Health Check to Your Auto Scaling Group in the *Amazon EC2 Auto Scaling User Guide*.

Topics

- Health Check Configuration
- Update the Health Check Configuration
- Check the Health of Your Instances
- Troubleshoot Health Checks

Health Check Configuration

A health configuration contains the information that a load balancer uses to determine the health state of the registered instances. The following table describes the health check configuration fields.

Field	Description
Ping Protocol	The protocol to use to connect with the instance. Valid values: TCP, HTTP, HTTPS, and SSL Console default: HTTP CLI/API default: TCP
Ping Port	The port to use to connect with the instance, as a `protocol:port` pair. If the load balancer fails to connect with the instance at the specified port within the configured response timeout period, the instance is considered unhealthy. Ping protocols: TCP, HTTP, HTTPS, and SSL Ping port range: 1 to 65535 Console default: HTTP:80 CLI/API default: TCP:80

Field	Description
Ping Path	The destination for the HTTP or HTTPS request. An HTTP or HTTPS GET request is issued to the instance on the ping port and the ping path. If the load balancer receives any response other than "200 OK" within the response timeout period, the instance is considered unhealthy. If the response includes a body, your application must either set the Content-Length header to a value greater than or equal to zero, or specify Transfer-Encoding with a value set to 'chunked'. Default: `/index.html`
Response Timeout	The amount of time to wait when receiving a response from the health check, in seconds. Valid values: 2 to 60 Default: 5
HealthCheck Interval	The amount of time between health checks of an individual instance, in seconds. Valid values: 5 to 300 Default: 30
Unhealthy Threshold	The number of consecutive failed health checks that must occur before declaring an EC2 instance unhealthy. Valid values: 2 to 10 Default: 2
Healthy Threshold	The number of consecutive successful health checks that must occur before declaring an EC2 instance healthy. Valid values: 2 to 10 Default: 10

The load balancer sends a request to each registered instance at the ping port and ping path every `Interval` seconds. An instance is considered healthy if it returns a 200 response code within the health check interval. If the health checks exceed the threshold for consecutive failed responses, the load balancer takes the instance out of service. When the health checks exceed the threshold for consecutive successful responses, the load balancer puts the instance back in service.

Update the Health Check Configuration

You can update the health check configuration for your load balancer at any time.

To update the health check configuration for your load balancer using the console

1. Open the Amazon EC2 console at https://console.aws.amazon.com/ec2/.
2. On the navigation pane, under **LOAD BALANCING**, choose **Load Balancers**.
3. Select your load balancer.
4. On the **Health Check** tab, choose **Edit Health Check**.
5. On the **Configure Health Check** page, update the configuration as needed.
6. Choose **Save**.

To update the health check configuration for your load balancer using the AWS CLI
Use the following configure-health-check command:

```
1 aws elb configure-health-check --load-balancer-name my-load-balancer --health-check Target=HTTP
    :80/ping,Interval=30,UnhealthyThreshold=2,HealthyThreshold=2,Timeout=3
```

Check the Health of Your Instances

You can check the health status of your registered instances.

To check the health status of your instances using the console

1. Open the Amazon EC2 console at https://console.aws.amazon.com/ec2/.

2. On the navigation pane, under **LOAD BALANCING**, choose **Load Balancers**.

3. Select your load balancer.

4. On the **Description** tab, **Status** indicates how many instances are in service.

5. On the **Instances** tab, the **Status** column indicates the status of each instance.

To check the health status of your instances using the AWS CLI
Use the following describe-instance-health command:

```
1  aws elb describe-instance-health --load-balancer-name my-load-balancer
```

Troubleshoot Health Checks

Your registered instances can fail the load balancer health check for several reasons. The most common reasons for failing a health check are where EC2 instances close connections to your load balancer or where the response from the EC2 instances times out. For information about potential causes and steps you can take to resolve failed health check issues, see Troubleshoot a Classic Load Balancer: Health Checks.

Configure Security Groups for Your Classic Load Balancer

A *security group* acts as a firewall that controls the traffic allowed to and from one or more instances. When you launch an EC2 instance, you can associate one or more security groups with the instance. For each security group, you add one or more rules to allow traffic. You can modify the rules for a security group at any time; the new rules are automatically applied to all instances associated with the security group. For more information, see Amazon EC2 Security Groups in the *Amazon EC2 User Guide for Linux Instances*.

There is a significant difference between the way Classic load balancers support security groups in EC2-Classic and in a VPC. In EC2-Classic, Elastic Load Balancing provides a special source security group that you can use to ensure that instances receive traffic only from your load balancer. You can't modify this source security group. In a VPC, you provide the security group for your load balancer, which enables you to choose the ports and protocols to allow. For example, you can open Internet Control Message Protocol (ICMP) connections for the load balancer to respond to ping requests (however, ping requests are not forwarded to any instances).

In both EC2-Classic and in a VPC, you must ensure that the security groups for your instances allow the load balancer to communicate with your instances on both the listener port and the health check port. In a VPC, your security groups and network access control lists (ACL) must allow traffic in both directions on these ports.

Topics

- Security Groups for Load Balancers in a VPC
- Security Groups for Instances in a VPC
- Network ACLs for Load Balancers in a VPC
- Security Groups for Instances in EC2-Classic

Security Groups for Load Balancers in a VPC

When you use the AWS Management Console to create a load balancer in a VPC, you can choose an existing security group for the VPC or create a new security group for the VPC. If you choose an existing security group, it must allow traffic in both directions to the listener and health check ports for the load balancer. If you choose to create a security group, the console automatically adds rules to allow all traffic on these ports.

[Nondefault VPC] If you use the AWS CLI or API create a load balancer in a nondefault VPC, but you don't specify a security group, your load balancer is automatically associated with the default security group for the VPC.

[Default VPC] If you use the AWS CLI or API to create a load balancer in your default VPC, you can't choose an existing security group for your load balancer. Instead, Elastic Load Balancing provides a security group with rules to allow all traffic on the ports specified for the load balancer. Elastic Load Balancing creates only one such security group per AWS account, with a name of the form default_elb_*id* (for example, `default_elb_fc5fbed3 -0405-3b7d-a328-ea290EXAMPLE`). Subsequent load balancers that you create in the default VPC also use this security group. Be sure to review the security group rules to ensure that they allow traffic on the listener and health check ports for the new load balancer. When you delete your load balancer, this security group is not deleted automatically.

If you add a listener to an existing load balancer, you must review your security groups to ensure they allow traffic on the new listener port in both directions.

Topics

- Recommended Rules for Load Balancer Security Groups
- Manage Security Groups Using the Console
- Manage Security Groups Using the AWS CLI

Recommended Rules for Load Balancer Security Groups

The security groups for your load balancers must allow them to communicate with your instances. The recommended rules depend on the type of load balancer (Internet-facing or internal).

Internet-facing Load Balancer: Recommended Rules

Inbound
Source
0.0.0.0/0
Outbound
Destination
instance security group
instance security group

Internal Load Balancer: Recommended Rules

Inbound
Source
VPC CIDR
Outbound
Destination
instance security group
instance security group

We also recommend that you allow inbound ICMP traffic to support Path MTU Discovery. For more information, see Path MTU Discovery in the *Amazon EC2 User Guide for Linux Instances*.

Manage Security Groups Using the Console

Use the following procedure to change the security groups associated with your load balancer in a VPC.

To update a security group assigned to your load balancer

1. Open the Amazon EC2 console at https://console.aws.amazon.com/ec2/.
2. On the navigation pane, under **LOAD BALANCING**, choose **Load Balancers**.
3. Select your load balancer.
4. On the **Description** tab, choose **Edit security groups**.
5. On the **Edit security groups** page, select or clear security groups as needed.
6. When you are finished, choose **Save**.

Manage Security Groups Using the AWS CLI

Use the following apply-security-groups-to-load-balancer command to associate a security group with a load balancer in a VPC. The specified security groups override the previously associated security groups.

```
1 aws elb apply-security-groups-to-load-balancer --load-balancer-name my-loadbalancer --security-
    groups sg-53fae93f
```

The following is an example response:

```
1 {
2   "SecurityGroups": [
3       "sg-53fae93f"
4   ]
5 }
```

Security Groups for Instances in a VPC

The security groups for your instances must allow them to communicate with the load balancer.

Instances: Recommended Rules

Inbound	
Source	
load balancer security group	
load balancer security group	

We also recommend that you allow inbound ICMP traffic to support Path MTU Discovery. For more information, see Path MTU Discovery in the *Amazon EC2 User Guide for Linux Instances*.

Network ACLs for Load Balancers in a VPC

The default network access control list (ACL) for the VPC allows all inbound and outbound traffic. If you create custom network ACLs, you must add rules that allow the load balancer and instances to communicate.

The recommended rules for the subnet for your load balancer depend on the type of load balancer (Internet-facing or internal).

Internet-Facing Load Balancer: Recommended Rules

Inbound	
Source	
0.0.0.0/0	
VPC CIDR	
Outbound	
Destination	
VPC CIDR	
VPC CIDR	
0.0.0.0/0	

Internal Load Balancer: Recommended Rules

Inbound	
Source	
VPC CIDR	
VPC CIDR	
Outbound	
Destination	
VPC CIDR	
VPC CIDR	
VPC CIDR	

The recommended rules for the subnet for your instances depend on whether the subnet is private or public. The following rules are for a private subnet. If your instances are in a public subnet, change the source and destination from the CIDR of the VPC to 0.0.0.0/0.

Instances: Recommended Rules

Inbound	
Source	
VPC CIDR	
VPC CIDR	
Outbound	
Destination	
VPC CIDR	

Security Groups for Instances in EC2-Classic

To allow communication between your load balancer and your instances launched in EC2-Classic, create an inbound rule for the security group for your instances that allows inbound traffic from either all IP addresses (using the 0.0.0.0/0 CIDR block) or only from the load balancer (using the source security group provided by Elastic Load Balancing).

Use the following procedure to lock down traffic between your load balancer and your instances in EC2-Classic.

To lock down traffic between your load balancer and instances using the console

1. Open the Amazon EC2 console at https://console.aws.amazon.com/ec2/.

2. On the navigation pane, under **LOAD BALANCING**, choose **Load Balancers**.

3. Select your load balancer.

4. On the **Description** tab, copy the name of the source security group.

    Security

    Source Security Group: `amazon-elb/amazon-elb-sg`
    Owner Alias: amazon-elb
    Group Name: amazon-elb-sg

5. On the **Instances** tab, select the instance ID of one of the instances registered with your load balancer.

6. On the **Description** tab, for **Security groups**, select the name of the security group.

7. On the **Inbound** tab, choose **Edit, Add Rule**.

8. From the **Type** column, select the protocol type. The **Protocol** and **Port Range** columns are populated. From the **Source** column, select Custom IP and then paste the name of the source security group that you copied earlier (for example, amazon-elb/amazon-elb-sg).

9. (Optional) If your security group has rules that are less restrictive than the rule that you just added, remove the less restrictive rule using its delete icon.

To lock down traffic between your load balancer and instances using the AWS CLI

1. Use the following describe-load-balancers command to display the name and owner of the source security group for your load balancer:

```
1 aws elb describe-load-balancers --load-balancer-name my-loadbalancer
```

30

The response includes the name and owner in the `SourceSecurityGroup` field. For example:

```
1  {
2      "LoadBalancerDescriptions": [
3          {
4              ...
5              "SourceSecurityGroup": {
6                  "OwnerAlias": "amazon-elb",
7                  "GroupName": "amazon-elb-sg"
8              }
9          }
10     ]
11 }
```

2. Add a rule to the security group for your instances as follows:

   1. If you do not know the name of the security group for your instances, use the following describe-instances command to get the name and ID of the security group for the specified instance:

      ```
      1 aws ec2 describe-instances --instance-ids i-315b7e51
      ```

      The response includes the name and ID of the security group in the `SecurityGroups` field. Make a note of the name of the security group; you'll use it in the next step.

   2. Use the following authorize-security-group-ingress command to add a rule to the security group for your instance to allow traffic from your load balancer:

      ```
      1 aws ec2 authorize-security-group-ingress --group-name my-security-group --source-
          security-group-name amazon-elb-sg  --source-security-group-owner-id amazon-elb
      ```

3. (Optional) Use the following describe-security-groups command to verify that the security group has the new rule:

   ```
   1 aws ec2 describe-security-groups --group-names my-security-group
   ```

   The response includes a `UserIdGroupPairs` data structure that lists the security groups that are granted permissions to access the instance.

```
1  {
2      "SecurityGroups": [
3          {
4              ...
5              "IpPermissions": [
6                  {
7                      "IpRanges": [],
8                      "FromPort": -1,
9                      "IpProtocol": "icmp",
10                     "ToPort": -1,
11                     "UserIdGroupPairs": [
12                         {
13                             "GroupName": "amazon-elb-sg",
14                             "GroupId": "sg-5a9c116a",
15                             "UserId": "amazon-elb"
16                         }
17                     ]
18                 },
19                 {
20                     "IpRanges": [],
```

```
21          "FromPort": 1,
22          "IpProtocol": "tcp",
23          "ToPort": 65535,
24          "UserIdGroupPairs": [
25              {
26                  "GroupName": "amazon-elb-sg",
27                  "GroupId": "sg-5a9c116a",
28                  "UserId": "amazon-elb"
29              }
30          ]
31      },
32      {
33          "IpRanges": [],
34          "FromPort": 1,
35          "IpProtocol": "udp",
36          "ToPort": 65535,
37          "UserIdGroupPairs": [
38              {
39                  "GroupName": "amazon-elb-sg",
40                  "GroupId": "sg-5a9c116a",
41                  "UserId": "amazon-elb"
42              }
43          ]
44      },
45      . . .
46 }
```

4. (Optional) If your security group has rules that are less restrictive than the rule you just added, use the revoke-security-group-ingress command to remove the less restrictive rules. For example, the following command removes a rule that allows TCP traffic from everyone (CIDR range 0.0.0.0/0):

```
1 aws ec2 revoke-security-group-ingress --group-name my-security-group --protocol tcp --port
    80 --cidr 0.0.0.0/0
```

Add or Remove Availability Zones for Your Load Balancer in EC2-Classic

When you add an Availability Zone to your load balancer, Elastic Load Balancing creates a load balancer node in the Availability Zone. Load balancer nodes accept traffic from clients and forward requests to the healthy registered instances in one or more Availability Zones.

You can set up your load balancer in EC2-Classic to distribute incoming requests across EC2 instances in a single Availability Zone or multiple Availability Zones. First, launch EC2 instances in all the Availability Zones that you plan to use. Next, register these instances with your load balancer. Finally, add the Availability Zones to your load balancer. After you add an Availability Zone, the load balancer starts routing requests to the registered instances in that Availability Zone. Note that you can modify the Availability Zones for your load balancer at any time.

By default, the load balancer routes requests evenly across its Availability Zones. To route requests evenly across the registered instances in the Availability Zones, enable cross-zone load balancing. For more information, see Configure Cross-Zone Load Balancing for Your Classic Load Balancer.

You might want to remove an Availability Zone from your load balancer temporarily when it has no healthy registered instances or when you want to troubleshoot or update the registered instances. After you've removed an Availability Zone, the load balancer stops routing requests to the registered instances in this Availability Zone but continues to route requests to the registered instances in the remaining Availability Zones.

If your load balancer is in a VPC, see Add or Remove Subnets for Your Classic Load Balancer in a VPC.

Topics

- Add an Availability Zone
- Remove an Availability Zone

Add an Availability Zone

You can expand the availability of your application to an additional Availability Zone. Register the instances in this Availability Zone with the load balancer, then add the Availability Zone. For more information, see Register or Deregister EC2 Instances for Your Classic Load Balancer.

To add an Availability Zone using the console

1. Open the Amazon EC2 console at https://console.aws.amazon.com/ec2/.

2. On the navigation pane, under **LOAD BALANCING**, choose **Load Balancers**.

3. Select your load balancer.

4. On the **Instances** tab, choose **Edit Availability Zones**.

5. On the **Add and Remove Availability Zones** page, select the Availability Zone.

6. Choose **Save**.

To add an Availability Zone using the AWS CLI
Use the following enable-availability-zones-for-load-balancer command to add an Availability Zone:

```
1 aws elb enable-availability-zones-for-load-balancer --load-balancer-name my-loadbalancer --
    availability-zones us-west-2b
```

The response lists all Availability Zones for the load balancer. For example:

```
1 {
2   "AvailabilityZones": [
3     "us-west-2a",
```

```
4       "us-west-2b"
5   ]
6 }
```

Remove an Availability Zone

You can remove an Availability Zone from your load balancer. Note that after you remove an Availability Zone, the instances in that Availability Zone remain registered with the load balancer. For more information, see Register or Deregister EC2 Instances for Your Classic Load Balancer.

To remove an Availability Zone using the console

1. Open the Amazon EC2 console at https://console.aws.amazon.com/ec2/.

2. On the navigation pane, under **LOAD BALANCING**, choose **Load Balancers**.

3. Select your load balancer.

4. On the **Instances** tab, choose **Edit Availability Zones**.

5. On the **Add and Remove Availability Zones** page, clear the Availability Zone.

6. Choose **Save**.

To remove an Availability Zone using the AWS CLI
Use the following disable-availability-zones-for-load-balancer command:

```
1 aws elb disable-availability-zones-for-load-balancer --load-balancer-name my-loadbalancer --
    availability-zones us-west-2a
```

The response lists the remaining Availability Zones for the load balancer. For example:

```
1 {
2     "AvailabilityZones": [
3         "us-west-2b"
4     ]
5 }
```

Add or Remove Subnets for Your Classic Load Balancer in a VPC

When you add a subnet to your load balancer, Elastic Load Balancing creates a load balancer node in the Availability Zone. Load balancer nodes accept traffic from clients and forward requests to the healthy registered instances in one or more Availability Zones. For load balancers in a VPC, we recommend that you add one subnet per Availability Zone for at least two Availability Zones. This improves the availability of your load balancer. Note that you can modify the subnets for your load balancer at any time.

Select subnets from the same Availability Zones as your instances. If your load balancer is an Internet-facing load balancer, you must select public subnets in order for your back-end instances to receive traffic from the load balancer (even if the back-end instances are in private subnets). If your load balancer is an internal load balancer, we recommend that you select private subnets. For more information about subnets for your load balancer, see Prepare Your VPC and EC2 Instances.

After you add a subnet, the load balancer starts routing requests to the registered instances in the corresponding Availability Zone. By default, the load balancer routes requests evenly across the Availability Zones for its subnets. To route requests evenly across the registered instances in the Availability Zones for its subnets, enable cross-zone load balancing. For more information, see Configure Cross-Zone Load Balancing for Your Classic Load Balancer.

You might want to remove a subnet from your load balancer temporarily when its Availability Zone has no healthy registered instances, or when you want to troubleshoot or update the registered instances. After you've removed a subnet, the load balancer stops routing requests to the registered instances in its Availability Zone, but continues to route requests to the registered instances in the Availability Zones for the remaining subnets.

If your load balancer is in EC2-Classic, see Add or Remove Availability Zones for Your Load Balancer in EC2-Classic.

Topics

- Requirements
- Add a Subnet
- Remove a Subnet

Requirements

When you update the subnets for your load balancer, you must meet the following requirements:

- The load balancer must have at least one subnet at all times.
- You can add at most one subnet per Availability Zone.

Because there are separate APIs to add and remove subnets from a load balancer, you must consider the order of operations carefully when swapping the current subnets for new subnets in order to meet these requirements. Also, you must temporarily add a subnet from another Availability Zone if you need to swap all subnets for your load balancer. For example, if your load balancer has a single Availability Zone and you need to swap its subnet for another subnet, you must first add a subnet from a second Availability Zone. Then you can remove the subnet from the original Availability Zone (without going below one subnet), add a new subnet from the original Availability Zone (without exceeding one subnet per Availability Zone), and then remove the subnet from the second Availability Zone (if it is only needed to perform the swap).

Add a Subnet

You can expand the availability of your load balancer to an additional subnet. Register the instances in this subnet with the load balancer, then attach a subnet to the load balancer that is from the same Availability Zone as the instances. For more information, see Register or Deregister EC2 Instances for Your Classic Load Balancer.

To add a subnet to your load balancer using the console

1. Open the Amazon EC2 console at https://console.aws.amazon.com/ec2/.

2. On the navigation pane, under **LOAD BALANCING**, choose **Load Balancers**.

3. Select your load balancer.

4. In the bottom pane, select the **Instances** tab.

5. Choose **Edit Availability Zones**.

6. For **Available Subnets**, select the subnet using its add (+) icon. The subnet is moved under **Selected subnets**.

   Note that you can select at most one subnet per Availability Zone. If you select a subnet from an Availability Zone where there is already an selected subnet, this subnet replaces the currently selected subnet for the Availability Zone.

7. Choose **Save**.

To add a subnet to your load balancer using the CLI

Use the following attach-load-balancer-to-subnets command to add two subnets to your load balancer:

```
1 aws elb attach-load-balancer-to-subnets --load-balancer-name my-load-balancer --subnet-
    dea770a9 subnet-fb14f6a2
```

The response lists all subnets for the load balancer. For example:

```
1 {
2     "Subnets": [
3         "subnet-5c11033e",
4         "subnet-dea770a9",
5         "subnet-fb14f6a2"
6     ]
7 }
```

Remove a Subnet

You can remove a subnet from your load balancer. Note that after you remove a subnet, the instances in that subnet remain registered with the load balancer. For more information, see Register or Deregister EC2 Instances for Your Classic Load Balancer.

To remove a subnet using the console

1. Open the Amazon EC2 console at https://console.aws.amazon.com/ec2/.

2. On the navigation pane, under **LOAD BALANCING**, choose **Load Balancers**.

3. Select your load balancer.

4. In the bottom pane, select the **Instances** tab.

5. Choose **Edit Availability Zones**.

6. For **Selected subnets**, remove the subnet using its delete (-) icon. The subnet is moved under **Available Subnets**.

7. Choose **Save**.

To remove a subnet using the AWS CLI

Use the following detach-load-balancer-from-subnets command to remove the specified subnets from the specified load balancer:

```
1 aws elb detach-load-balancer-from-subnets --load-balancer-name my-loadbalancer --subnet
    -450f5127
```

The response lists the remaining subnets for the load balancer. For example:

```
1 {
2     "Subnets": [
3         "subnet-15aaab61"
4     ]
5 }
```

Register or Deregister EC2 Instances for Your Classic Load Balancer

Registering an EC2 instance adds it to your load balancer. The load balancer continuously monitors the health of registered instances in its enabled Availability Zones, and routes requests to the instances that are healthy. If demand on your instances increases, you can register additional instances with the load balancer to handle the demand.

Deregistering an EC2 instance removes it from your load balancer. The load balancer stops routing requests to an instance as soon as it is deregistered. If demand decreases, or you need to service your instances, you can deregister instances from the load balancer. An instance that is deregistered remains running, but no longer receives traffic from the load balancer, and you can register it with the load balancer again when you are ready.

When you deregister an instance, Elastic Load Balancing waits until in-flight requests have completed if connection draining is enabled. For more information, see Configure Connection Draining for Your Classic Load Balancer.

If your load balancer is attached to an Auto Scaling group, instances in the group are automatically registered with the load balancer. If you detach a load balancer from your Auto Scaling group, the instances in the group are deregistered.

Elastic Load Balancing registers your EC2 instance with your load balancer using its IP address.

[EC2-VPC] When you register an instance with an elastic network interface (ENI) attached, the load balancer routes requests to the primary IP address of the primary interface (eth0) of the instance.

Topics

- Prerequisites
- Register an Instance
- Deregister an Instance

Prerequisites

The instance must be a running instance in the same network as the load balancer (EC2-Classic or the same VPC). If you have EC2-Classic instances and a load balancer in a VPC with ClassicLink enabled, you can link the EC2-Classic instances to that VPC and then register them with a load balancer in the VPC.

Register an Instance

When you are ready, register your instance with your load balancer. If the instance is an in Availability Zone that is enabled for the load balancer, the instance is ready to receive traffic from the load balancer as soon as it passes the required number of health checks.

To register your instances using the console

1. Open the Amazon EC2 console at https://console.aws.amazon.com/ec2/.
2. On the navigation pane, under **LOAD BALANCING**, choose **Load Balancers**.
3. Select your load balancer.
4. In the bottom pane, select the **Instances** tab.
5. Choose **Edit Instances**.
6. Select the instance to register with your load balancer.
7. Choose **Save**.

To register your instances using the AWS CLI
Use the following register-instances-with-load-balancer command:

```
1 aws elb register-instances-with-load-balancer --load-balancer-name my-loadbalancer --instances i
    -4e05f721
```

The following is an example response that lists the instances registered with the load balancer:

```
 1 {
 2     "Instances": [
 3         {
 4             "InstanceId": "i-315b7e51"
 5         },
 6         {
 7             "InstanceId": "i-4e05f721"
 8         }
 9     ]
10 }
```

Deregister an Instance

You can deregister an instance from your load balancer if you no longer need the capacity or if you need to service the instance.

If your load balancer is attached to an Auto Scaling group, detaching the instance from the group also deregisters it from the load balancer. For more information, see Detach EC2 Instances From Your Auto Scaling Group in the *Amazon EC2 Auto Scaling User Guide*.

To deregister your instances using the console

1. Open the Amazon EC2 console at https://console.aws.amazon.com/ec2/.

2. On the navigation pane, under **LOAD BALANCING**, choose **Load Balancers**.

3. Select your load balancer.

4. In the bottom pane, select the **Instances** tab.

5. In **Actions** column for the instance, choose **Remove from Load Balancer**.

6. When prompted for confirmation, choose **Yes, Remove**.

To deregister your instances using the AWS CLI

Use the following deregister-instances-from-load-balancer command:

```
1 aws elb deregister-instances-from-load-balancer --load-balancer-name my-loadbalancer --instances
    i-4e05f721
```

The following is an example response that lists the remaining instances registered with the load balancer:

```
1 {
2     "Instances": [
3         {
4             "InstanceId": "i-315b7e51"
5         }
6     ]
7 }
```

Listeners for Your Classic Load Balancer

Before you start using Elastic Load Balancing, you must configure one or more *listeners* for your Classic Load Balancer. A listener is a process that checks for connection requests. It is configured with a protocol and a port for front-end (client to load balancer) connections, and a protocol and a port for back-end (load balancer to back-end instance) connections.

Elastic Load Balancing supports the following protocols:

- HTTP
- HTTPS (secure HTTP)
- TCP
- SSL (secure TCP)

The HTTPS protocol uses the SSL protocol to establish secure connections over the HTTP layer. You can also use the SSL protocol to establish secure connections over the TCP layer.

If the front-end connection uses TCP or SSL, then your back-end connections can use either TCP or SSL. If the front-end connection uses HTTP or HTTPS, then your back-end connections can use either HTTP or HTTPS.

Back-end instances can listen on ports 1-65535.

Load balancers can listen on the following ports:

- [EC2-VPC] 1-65535
- [EC2-Classic] 25, 80, 443, 465, 587, 1024-65535

Topics

- Protocols
- HTTPS/SSL Listeners
- Listener Configurations for Classic Load Balancers
- HTTP Headers and Classic Load Balancers

Protocols

Communication for a typical web application goes through layers of hardware and software. Each layer provides a specific communication function. The control over the communication function is passed from one layer to the next, in sequence. The Open System Interconnection (OSI) defines a model framework for implementing a standard format for communication, called a *protocol*, in these layers. For more information, see OSI model in Wikipedia.

When you use Elastic Load Balancing, you need a basic understanding of layer 4 and layer 7. Layer 4 is the transport layer that describes the Transmission Control Protocol (TCP) connection between the client and your back-end instance, through the load balancer. Layer 4 is the lowest level that is configurable for your load balancer. Layer 7 is the application layer that describes the use of Hypertext Transfer Protocol (HTTP) and HTTPS (secure HTTP) connections from clients to the load balancer and from the load balancer to your back-end instance.

The Secure Sockets Layer (SSL) protocol is primarily used to encrypt confidential data over insecure networks such as the Internet. The SSL protocol establishes a secure connection between a client and the back-end server, and ensures that all the data passed between your client and your server is private and integral.

TCP/SSL Protocol

When you use TCP (layer 4) for both front-end and back-end connections, your load balancer forwards the request to the back-end instances without modifying the headers. After your load balancer receives the request, it attempts to open a TCP connection to the back-end instance on the port specified in the listener configuration.

Because load balancers intercept traffic between clients and your back-end instances, the access logs for your back-end instance contain the IP address of the load balancer instead of the originating client. You can enable Proxy Protocol, which adds a header with the connection information of the client, such as the source IP address, destination IP address, and port numbers. The header is then sent to the back-end instance as a part of the request. You can parse the first line in the request to retrieve the connection information. For more information, see Configure Proxy Protocol Support for Your Classic Load Balancer.

Using this configuration, you do not receive cookies for session stickiness or X-Forwarded headers.

HTTP/HTTPS Protocol

When you use HTTP (layer 7) for both front-end and back-end connections, your load balancer parses the headers in the request and terminates the connection before sending the request to the back-end instances.

For every registered and healthy instance behind an HTTP/HTTPS load balancer, Elastic Load Balancing opens and maintains one or more TCP connections. These connections ensure that there is always an established connection ready to receive HTTP/HTTPS requests.

The HTTP requests and HTTP responses use header fields to send information about HTTP messages. Elastic Load Balancing supports X-Forwarded-For headers. Because load balancers intercept traffic between clients and servers, your server access logs contain only the IP address of the load balancer. To see the IP address of the client, use the X-Forwarded-For request header. For more information, see X-Forwarded-For.

When you use HTTP/HTTPS, you can enable sticky sessions on your load balancer. A sticky session binds a user's session to a specific back-end instance. This ensures that all requests coming from the user during the session are sent to the same back-end instance. For more information, see Configure Sticky Sessions for Your Classic Load Balancer.

Not all HTTP extensions are supported in the load balancer. You may need to use a TCP listener if the load balancer is not able to terminate the request due to unexpected methods, response codes, or other non-standard HTTP 1.0/1.1 implementations.

HTTPS/SSL Listeners

You can create a load balancer with the following security features.

SSL Server Certificates

If you use HTTPS or SSL for your front-end connections, you must deploy an X.509 certificate (SSL server certificate) on your load balancer. The load balancer decrypts requests from clients before sending them to the back-end instances (known as *SSL termination*). For more information, see SSL/TLS Certificates for Classic Load Balancers.

If you don't want the load balancer to handle the SSL termination (known as *SSL offloading*), you can use TCP for both the front-end and back-end connections, and deploy certificates on the registered instances handling requests.

SSL Negotiation

Elastic Load Balancing provides predefined SSL negotiation configurations that are used for SSL negotiation when a connection is established between a client and your load balancer. The SSL negotiation configurations provide compatibility with a broad range of clients and use high-strength cryptographic algorithms called *ciphers*. However, some use cases might require all data on the network to be encrypted and allow only specific ciphers. Some security compliance standards (such as PCI, SOX, and so on) might require a specific set of protocols and ciphers from clients to ensure that the security standards are met. In such cases, you can create a custom SSL negotiation configuration, based on your specific requirements. Your ciphers and protocols should take effect within 30 seconds. For more information, see SSL Negotiation Configurations for Classic Load Balancers.

Back-End Server Authentication

If you use HTTPS or SSL for your back-end connections, you can enable authentication of your registered instances. You can then use the authentication process to ensure that the instances accept only encrypted communication, and to ensure that each registered instance has the correct public key.

For more information, see Configure Back-end Server Authentication.

Listener Configurations for Classic Load Balancers

The following tables summarizes the listener settings that you can use to configure your Classic Load Balancers.

HTTP/HTTPS Load Balancer

Use Case	Front-End Protocol	Front-End Options	Back-End Protocol	Back-End Options	Notes
Basic HTTP load balancer	HTTP	NA	HTTP	NA	[See the AWS documentation website for more details]
Secure website or application using Elastic Load Balancing to offload SSL decryption	HTTPS	SSL negotiation	HTTP	NA	[See the AWS documentation website for more details]
Secure website or application using end-to-end encryption	HTTPS	SSL negotiation	HTTPS	Back-end authentication	[See the AWS documentation website for more details]

TCP/SSL Load Balancer

Use Case	Front-End Protocol	Front-End Options	Back-End Protocol	Back-End Options	Notes
Basic TCP load balancer	TCP	NA	TCP	NA	[See the AWS documentation website for more details]
Secure website or application using Elastic Load Balancing to offload SSL decryption	SSL	SSL negotiation	TCP	NA	[See the AWS documentation website for more details]
Secure website or application using end-to-end encryption with Elastic Load Balancing	SSL	SSL negotiation	SSL	Back-end authentication	[See the AWS documentation website for more details]

43

HTTP Headers and Classic Load Balancers

HTTP requests and HTTP responses use header fields to send information about the HTTP messages. Header fields are colon-separated name-value pairs that are separated by a carriage return (CR) and a line feed (LF). A standard set of HTTP header fields is defined in RFC 2616, Message Headers. There are also non-standard HTTP headers available that are widely used by the applications. Some of the non-standard HTTP headers have a `X-Forwarded` prefix. Classic Load Balancers support the following `X-Forwarded` headers.

For more information about HTTP connections, see Request Routing in the *Elastic Load Balancing User Guide*.

Prerequisites

- Confirm that your listener settings support the X-Forwarded headers. For more information, see Listener Configurations for Classic Load Balancers.
- Configure your web server to log client IP addresses.

Topics

- X-Forwarded-For
- X-Forwarded-Proto
- X-Forwarded-Port

X-Forwarded-For

The `X-Forwarded-For` request header helps you identify the IP address of a client when you use an HTTP or HTTPS load balancer. Because load balancers intercept traffic between clients and servers, your server access logs contain only the IP address of the load balancer. To see the IP address of the client, use the `X-Forwarded-For` request header. Elastic Load Balancing stores the IP address of the client in the `X-Forwarded-For` request header and passes the header to your server.

The `X-Forwarded-For` request header takes the following form:

```
1 X-Forwarded-For: client-ip-address
```

The following is an example `X-Forwarded-For` request header for a client with an IP address of 203.0.113.7.

```
1 X-Forwarded-For: 203.0.113.7
```

The following is an example `X-Forwarded-For` request header for a client with an IPv6 address of 2001:DB8 ::21f:5bff:febf:ce22:8a2e.

```
1 X-Forwarded-For: 2001:DB8::21f:5bff:febf:ce22:8a2e
```

If a request from a client already contains an `X-Forwarded-For` header, Elastic Load Balancing appends the IP address of the client at the end of the header value. In this case, the last IP address in the list is the IP address of the client. For example, the following header contains two IP addresses added by the client, which might not be trustworthy, plus the client IP address added by Elastic Load Balancing:

```
1 X-Forwarded-For: ip-address-1, ip-address-2, client-ip-address
```

X-Forwarded-Proto

The `X-Forwarded-Proto` request header helps you identify the protocol (HTTP or HTTPS) that a client used to connect to your load balancer. Your server access logs contain only the protocol used between the server and the load balancer; they contain no information about the protocol used between the client and the load balancer. To determine the protocol used between the client and the load balancer, use the `X-Forwarded-Proto` request header. Elastic Load Balancing stores the protocol used between the client and the load balancer in the `X-Forwarded-Proto` request header and passes the header along to your server.

Your application or website can use the protocol stored in the `X-Forwarded-Proto` request header to render a response that redirects to the appropriate URL.

The `X-Forwarded-Proto` request header takes the following form:

```
1  X-Forwarded-Proto: originatingProtocol
```

The following example contains an `X-Forwarded-Proto` request header for a request that originated from the client as an HTTPS request:

```
1  X-Forwarded-Proto: https
```

X-Forwarded-Port

The `X-Forwarded-Port` request header helps you identify the port that the client used to connect to the load balancer.

HTTPS Listeners for Your Classic Load Balancer

You can create a load balancer that uses the SSL/TLS protocol for encrypted connections (also known as *SSL offload*). This feature enables traffic encryption between your load balancer and the clients that initiate HTTPS sessions, and for connections between your load balancer and your EC2 instances.

Elastic Load Balancing uses Secure Sockets Layer (SSL) negotiation configurations, known as *security policies*, to negotiate connections between the clients and the load balancer. When you use HTTPS/SSL for your front-end connections, you can use either a predefined security policy or a custom security policy. You must deploy an SSL certificate on your load balancer. The load balancer uses this certificate to terminate the connection and then decrypt requests from clients before sending them to the instances. The default security policy is always used for back-end connections. You can optionally choose to enable authentication on your instances.

Elastic Load Balancing does not support Server Name Indication (SNI) on your load balancer. You can use one of the following alternatives instead:

- Deploy one certificate on the load balancer, and add a Subject Alternative Name (SAN) for each additional website. SANs enable you to protect multiple host names using a single certificate. Check with your certificate provider for more information about the number of SANs they support per certificate and how to add and remove SANs.
- Use TCP listeners on port 443 for the front-end and back-end connections. The load balancer passes the request through, with the SNI certificate as is. You can handle the HTTPS termination from the EC2 instance.

Topics

- SSL/TLS Certificates for Classic Load Balancers
- SSL Negotiation Configurations for Classic Load Balancers
- Create a Classic Load Balancer with an HTTPS Listener
- Configure an HTTPS Listener for Your Classic Load Balancer
- Replace the SSL Certificate for Your Classic Load Balancer
- Update the SSL Negotiation Configuration of Your Classic Load Balancer

SSL/TLS Certificates for Classic Load Balancers

If you use HTTPS (SSL or TLS) for your front-end listener, you must deploy an SSL/TLS certificate on your load balancer. The load balancer uses the certificate to terminate the connection and then decrypt requests from clients before sending them to the instances.

The SSL and TLS protocols use an X.509 certificate (SSL/TLS server certificate) to authenticate both the client and the back-end application. An X.509 certificate is a digital form of identification issued by a certificate authority (CA) and contains identification information, a validity period, a public key, a serial number, and the digital signature of the issuer.

You can create a certificate using AWS Certificate Manager or a tool that supports the SSL and TLS protocols, such as OpenSSL. You will specify this certificate when you create or update an HTTPS listener for your load balancer. When you create a certificate for use with your load balancer, you must specify a domain name.

Create or Import an SSL/TLS Certificate Using AWS Certificate Manager

We recommend that you use AWS Certificate Manager (ACM) to create or import certificates for your load balancer. ACM integrates with Elastic Load Balancing so that you can deploy the certificate on your load balancer. To deploy a certificate on your load balancer, the certificate must be in the same region as the load balancer. For more information, see Request a Public Certificate or Importing Certificates in the *AWS Certificate Manager User Guide*.

To allow an IAM user to deploy the certificate on your load balancer using the AWS Management Console, you must allow access to the ACM `ListCertificates` API action. For more information, see Listing Certificates in the *AWS Certificate Manager User Guide*.

Important
ACM supports RSA certificates with a 4096 key length and EC certificates. However, you cannot install these certificates on your load balancer through integration with ACM. You must upload these certificates to IAM in order to use them with your load balancer.

Import an SSL/TLS Certificate Using IAM

If you are not using ACM, you can use SSL/TLS tools, such as OpenSSL, to create a certificate signing request (CSR), get the CSR signed by a CA to produce a certificate, and upload the certificate to AWS Identity and Access Management (IAM). For more information about uploading certificates to IAM, see Working with Server Certificates in the *IAM User Guide*.

SSL Negotiation Configurations for Classic Load Balancers

Elastic Load Balancing uses a Secure Socket Layer (SSL) negotiation configuration, known as a *security policy*, to negotiate SSL connections between a client and the load balancer. A security policy is a combination of SSL protocols, SSL ciphers, and the Server Order Preference option. For more information about configuring an SSL connection for your load balancer, see Listeners for Your Classic Load Balancer.

Topics

- Security Policies
- SSL Protocols
- Server Order Preference
- SSL Ciphers
- Predefined SSL Security Policies for Classic Load Balancers

Security Policies

A security policy determines which ciphers and protocols are supported during SSL negotiations between a client and a load balancer. You can configure your Classic Load Balancers to use either predefined or custom security policies.

Note that a certificate provided by AWS Certificate Manager (ACM) contains an RSA public key. Therefore, you must include a cipher suite that uses RSA in your security policy if you use a certificate provided by ACM; otherwise, the TLS connection fails.

Predefined Security Policies

The names of the most recent predefined security policies includes version information based on the year and month that they were released. For example, the default predefined security policy is `ELBSecurityPolicy-2016-08`. Whenever a new predefined security policy is released, you can update your configuration to use it.

For information about the protocols and ciphers enabled for the predefined security policies, see Predefined SSL Security Policies.

Custom Security Policies

You can create a custom negotiation configuration with the ciphers and protocols that you need. For example, some security compliance standards (such as PCI and SOC) might require a specific set of protocols and ciphers to ensure that the security standards are met. In such cases, you can create a custom security policy to meet those standards.

For information about creating a custom security policy, see Update the SSL Negotiation Configuration of Your Classic Load Balancer.

SSL Protocols

The *SSL protocol* establishes a secure connection between a client and a server, and ensures that all the data passed between the client and your load balancer is private.

Secure Sockets Layer (SSL) and Transport Layer Security (TLS) are cryptographic protocols that are used to encrypt confidential data over insecure networks such as the Internet. The TLS protocol is a newer version of the SSL protocol. In the Elastic Load Balancing documentation, we refer to both SSL and TLS protocols as the SSL protocol.

SSL Protocols

The following versions of the SSL protocol are supported:

- TLS 1.2

- TLS 1.1
- TLS 1.0
- SSL 3.0

Deprecated SSL Protocol

If you previously enabled the SSL 2.0 protocol in a custom policy, we recommend that you update your security policy to the default predefined security policy.

Server Order Preference

Elastic Load Balancing supports the *Server Order Preference* option for negotiating connections between a client and a load balancer. During the SSL connection negotiation process, the client and the load balancer present a list of ciphers and protocols that they each support, in order of preference. By default, the first cipher on the client's list that matches any one of the load balancer's ciphers is selected for the SSL connection. If the load balancer is configured to support Server Order Preference, then the load balancer selects the first cipher in its list that is in the client's list of ciphers. This ensures that the load balancer determines which cipher is used for SSL connection. If you do not enable Server Order Preference, the order of ciphers presented by the client is used to negotiate connections between the client and the load balancer.

SSL Ciphers

An *SSL cipher* is an encryption algorithm that uses encryption keys to create a coded message. SSL protocols use several SSL ciphers to encrypt data over the Internet.

Note that a certificate provided by AWS Certificate Manager (ACM) contains an RSA public key. Therefore, you must include a cipher suite that uses RSA in your security policy if you use a certificate provided by ACM; otherwise, the TLS connection fails.

Elastic Load Balancing supports the following ciphers for use with Classic Load Balancers. A subset of these ciphers are used by the predefined SSL policies. All of these ciphers are available for use in a custom policy. We recommend that you use only the ciphers included in the default security policy (those with an asterisk). Many of the other ciphers are not secure and should be used at your own risk.

Ciphers

- ECDHE-ECDSA-AES128-GCM-SHA256 *
- ECDHE-RSA-AES128-GCM-SHA256 *
- ECDHE-ECDSA-AES128-SHA256 *
- ECDHE-RSA-AES128-SHA256 *
- ECDHE-ECDSA-AES128-SHA *
- ECDHE-RSA-AES128-SHA *
- DHE-RSA-AES128-SHA
- ECDHE-ECDSA-AES256-GCM-SHA384 *
- ECDHE-RSA-AES256-GCM-SHA384 *
- ECDHE-ECDSA-AES256-SHA384 *
- ECDHE-RSA-AES256-SHA384 *
- ECDHE-RSA-AES256-SHA *
- ECDHE-ECDSA-AES256-SHA *
- AES128-GCM-SHA256 *
- AES128-SHA256 *
- AES128-SHA *
- AES256-GCM-SHA384 *
- AES256-SHA256 *
- AES256-SHA *
- DHE-DSS-AES128-SHA

- CAMELLIA128-SHA
- EDH-RSA-DES-CBC3-SHA
- DES-CBC3-SHA
- ECDHE-RSA-RC4-SHA
- RC4-SHA
- ECDHE-ECDSA-RC4-SHA
- DHE-DSS-AES256-GCM-SHA384
- DHE-RSA-AES256-GCM-SHA384
- DHE-RSA-AES256-SHA256
- DHE-DSS-AES256-SHA256
- DHE-RSA-AES256-SHA
- DHE-DSS-AES256-SHA
- DHE-RSA-CAMELLIA256-SHA
- DHE-DSS-CAMELLIA256-SHA
- CAMELLIA256-SHA
- EDH-DSS-DES-CBC3-SHA
- DHE-DSS-AES128-GCM-SHA256
- DHE-RSA-AES128-GCM-SHA256
- DHE-RSA-AES128-SHA256
- DHE-DSS-AES128-SHA256
- DHE-RSA-CAMELLIA128-SHA
- DHE-DSS-CAMELLIA128-SHA
- ADH-AES128-GCM-SHA256
- ADH-AES128-SHA
- ADH-AES128-SHA256
- ADH-AES256-GCM-SHA384
- ADH-AES256-SHA
- ADH-AES256-SHA256
- ADH-CAMELLIA128-SHA
- ADH-CAMELLIA256-SHA
- ADH-DES-CBC3-SHA
- ADH-DES-CBC-SHA
- ADH-RC4-MD5
- ADH-SEED-SHA
- DES-CBC-SHA
- DHE-DSS-SEED-SHA
- DHE-RSA-SEED-SHA
- EDH-DSS-DES-CBC-SHA
- EDH-RSA-DES-CBC-SHA
- IDEA-CBC-SHA
- RC4-MD5
- SEED-SHA
- DES-CBC3-MD5
- DES-CBC-MD5
- RC2-CBC-MD5
- PSK-AES256-CBC-SHA
- PSK-3DES-EDE-CBC-SHA
- KRB5-DES-CBC3-SHA
- KRB5-DES-CBC3-MD5
- PSK-AES128-CBC-SHA
- PSK-RC4-SHA
- KRB5-RC4-SHA
- KRB5-RC4-MD5
- KRB5-DES-CBC-SHA

- KRB5-DES-CBC-MD5
- EXP-EDH-RSA-DES-CBC-SHA
- EXP-EDH-DSS-DES-CBC-SHA
- EXP-ADH-DES-CBC-SHA
- EXP-DES-CBC-SHA
- EXP-RC2-CBC-MD5
- EXP-KRB5-RC2-CBC-SHA
- EXP-KRB5-DES-CBC-SHA
- EXP-KRB5-RC2-CBC-MD5
- EXP-KRB5-DES-CBC-MD5
- EXP-ADH-RC4-MD5
- EXP-RC4-MD5
- EXP-KRB5-RC4-SHA
- EXP-KRB5-RC4-MD5

* These are the recommended ciphers included in the default security policy.

Predefined SSL Security Policies for Classic Load Balancers

We recommend that you always use the default predefined security policy, ELBSecurityPolicy-2016-08. For more information about updating the SSL negotiation configuration for your HTTPS/SSL listener, see Update the SSL Negotiation Configuration of Your Classic Load Balancer.

The RSA- and DSA-based ciphers are specific to the signing algorithm used to create SSL certificate. Make sure to create an SSL certificate using the signing algorithm that is based on the ciphers that are enabled for your security policy.

The following table describes the most recent predefined security policies, including their enabled SSL protocols and SSL ciphers. If you select a policy that is enabled for Server Order Preference, the load balancer uses the ciphers in the order that they are specified in this table to negotiate connections between the client and load balancer. Otherwise, the load balancer uses the ciphers in the order that they are presented by the client.

Security Policy	2016-08	TLS-1-1-2017-01	TLS-1-2-2017-01	2015-05	2015-03	2015-02
SSL Protocols						
Protocol-TLSv1						
Protocol-TLSv1.1						
Protocol-TLSv1.2						
SSL Options						
Server Order Preference						
SSL Ciphers						
ECDHE-ECDSA-AES128-GCM-SHA256						
ECDHE-RSA-AES128-GCM-SHA256						
ECDHE-ECDSA-AES128-SHA2						
ECDHE-RSA-AES128-SHA2						
ECDHE-ECDSA-AES128-SHA						
ECDHE-RSA-AES128-SHA						
DHE-RSA-AES128-SHA						
ECDHE-ECDSA-AES256-GCM-SHA384						

Security Policy	2016-08	TLS-1-1-2017-01	TLS-1-2-2017-01	2015-05	2015-03	2015-02
ECDHE-RSA-AES256-GCM-SHA384						
ECDHE-ECDSA-AES256-SHA3						
ECDHE-RSA-AES256-SHA3						
ECDHE-RSA-AES256-SHA						
ECDHE-ECDSA-AES256-SHA						
AES128-GCM-SHA256						
AES128-SHA2						
AES128-SHA						
AES256-GCM-SHA384						
AES256-SHA2						
AES256-SHA						
DHE-DSS-AES128-SHA						
DES-CBC3-SHA						

Predefined Security Policies

The following are the predefined security policies for Classic Load Balancers. To describe a predefined policy, use the describe-load-balancer-policies command.

- ELBSecurityPolicy-2016-08
- ELBSecurityPolicy-TLS-1-2-2017-01
- ELBSecurityPolicy-TLS-1-1-2017-01
- ELBSecurityPolicy-2015-05
- ELBSecurityPolicy-2015-03
- ELBSecurityPolicy-2015-02
- ELBSecurityPolicy-2014-10
- ELBSecurityPolicy-2014-01
- ELBSecurityPolicy-2011-08
- ELBSample-ELBDefaultNegotiationPolicy or ELBSample-ELBDefaultCipherPolicy
- ELBSample-OpenSSLDefaultNegotiationPolicy or ELBSample-OpenSSLDefaultCipherPolicy

Create a Classic Load Balancer with an HTTPS Listener

A load balancer takes requests from clients and distributes them across the EC2 instances that are registered with the load balancer.

You can create a load balancer that listens on both the HTTP (80) and HTTPS (443) ports. If you specify that the HTTPS listener sends requests to the instances on port 80, the load balancer terminates the requests and communication from the load balancer to the instances is not encrypted. If the HTTPS listener sends requests to the instances on port 443, communication from the load balancer to the instances is encrypted.

If your load balancer uses an encrypted connection to communicate with the instances, you can optionally enable authentication of the instances. This ensures that the load balancer communicates with an instance only if its public key matches the key that you specified to the load balancer for this purpose.

For information about adding an HTTPS listener to an existing load balancer, see Configure an HTTPS Listener for Your Classic Load Balancer.

Topics

- Prerequisites
- Create an HTTPS/SSL Load Balancer Using the Console
- Create an HTTPS/SSL Load Balancer Using the AWS CLI

Prerequisites

Before you get started, be sure that you've met the following prerequisites:

- Complete the steps in Prepare Your VPC and EC2 Instances.
- Launch the EC2 instances that you plan to register with your load balancer. The security groups for these instances must allow traffic from the load balancer.
- The EC2 instances must respond to the target of the health check with an HTTP status code 200. For more information, see Configure Health Checks for Your Classic Load Balancer.
- If you plan to enable the keep-alive option on your EC2 instances, we recommend that you set the keep-alive settings to at least the idle timeout settings of your load balancer. If you want to ensure that the load balancer is responsible for closing the connections to your instance, make sure that the value set on your instance for the keep-alive time is greater than the idle timeout setting on your load balancer. For more information, see Configure the Idle Connection Timeout for Your Classic Load Balancer.
- If you create a secure listener, you must deploy an SSL server certificate on your load balancer. The load balancer uses the certificate to terminate and then decrypt requests before sending them to the instances. If you don't have an SSL certificate, you can create one. For more information, see SSL/TLS Certificates for Classic Load Balancers.

Create an HTTPS/SSL Load Balancer Using the Console

To create an HTTPS/SSL load balancer, complete the following tasks.

Topics

- Step 1: Define Your Load Balancer
- Step 2: Assign Security Groups to Your Load Balancer in a VPC
- Step 3: Configure Security Settings
- Step 4: Configure Health Checks
- Step 5: Register EC2 Instances with Your Load Balancer
- Step 6: Tag Your Load Balancer (Optional)
- Step 7: Create and Verify Your Load Balancer
- Step 8: Delete Your Load Balancer (Optional)

Step 1: Define Your Load Balancer

First, provide some basic configuration information for your load balancer, such as a name, a network, and one or more listeners.

A *listener* is a process that checks for connection requests. It is configured with a protocol and a port for front-end (client to load balancer) connections and a protocol and a port for back-end (load balancer to instance) connections. For information about the ports, protocols, and listener configurations supported by Elastic Load Balancing, see Listeners for Your Classic Load Balancer.

In this example, you configure two listeners for your load balancer. The first listener accepts HTTP requests on port 80 and sends them to the instances on port 80 using HTTP. The second listener accepts HTTPS requests on port 443 and sends them to the instances using HTTP on port 80 (or using HTTPS on port 443 if you want to configure back-end instance authentication).

To define your load balancer

1. Open the Amazon EC2 console at https://console.aws.amazon.com/ec2/.

2. On the navigation pane, under **LOAD BALANCING**, choose **Load Balancers**.

3. Choose **Create Load Balancer**.

4. For **Select load balancer type**, choose **Classic Load Balancer**.

5. For **Load Balancer name**, type a name for your load balancer.

   The name of your Classic Load Balancer must be unique within your set of Classic Load Balancers for the region, can have a maximum of 32 characters, can contain only alphanumeric characters and hyphens, and must not begin or end with a hyphen.

6. For **Create LB inside**, select the same network that you selected for your instances: EC2-Classic or a specific VPC.

7. [Default VPC] If you selected a default VPC and would like to choose the subnets for your load balancer, select **Enable advanced VPC configuration**.

8. For **Listener Configuration**, leave the default listener, and choose **Add** to add another listener. For **Load Balancer Protocol** for the new listener, select **HTTPS (Secure HTTP)**. This updates **Load Balancer Port**, **Instance Protocol**, and **Instance Port**.

   By default, **Instance Protocol** is HTTP and **Instance Port** is 80.

Load Balancer Protocol	Load Balancer Port	Instance Protocol	Instance Port	
HTTP ▾	80	HTTP ▾	80	✕
HTTPS (Secure HTTP) ▾	443	HTTP ▾	80	✕

   Add

   If you want to set up back-end instance authentication (later, in Step 3: Configure Security Settings), change the instance protocol to **HTTPS (Secure HTTP)**. This also updates **Instance Port**.

Load Balancer Protocol	Load Balancer Port	Instance Protocol	Instance Port	
HTTP ▾	80	HTTP ▾	80	✕
HTTPS (Secure HTTP) ▾	443	HTTPS (Secure HTTP) ▾	443	✕

   Add

9. [EC2-VPC] For **Available subnets**, select at least one available subnet using its add icon. The subnets are moved under **Selected subnets**. To improve the availability of your load balancer, select subnets from more than one Availability Zone. **Note**
   If you selected EC2-Classic as your network, or you have a default VPC but did not select **Enable advanced VPC configuration**, you do not see the user interface to select subnets.

   You can add at most one subnet per Availability Zone. If you select a second subnet from an Availability Zone where there is already a selected subnet, this subnet replaces the currently selected subnet for that Availability Zone.

Available subnets

Actions	Availability Zone	Subnet ID	Subnet CIDR	Name
➕	us-west-2c	subnet-cb663da2	10.0.1.0/24	
➕	us-west-2c	subnet-c9663da0	10.0.0.0/24	

Selected subnets

Actions	Availability Zone	Subnet ID	Subnet CIDR	Name
➖	us-west-2a	subnet-e4f33493	10.0.2.0/24	
➖	us-west-2b	subnet-5264e837	10.0.3.0/24	

10. Choose **Next: Assign Security Groups**.

Step 2: Assign Security Groups to Your Load Balancer in a VPC

If you selected a VPC as your network, you must assign your load balancer a security group that allows inbound traffic to the ports that you specified for your load balancer and the health checks for your load balancer.

Note
If you selected EC2-Classic as your network, you can continue to the next step. By default, Elastic Load Balancing provides a security group for load balancers in EC2-Classic.

To assign security group to your load balancer

1. On the **Assign Security Groups** page, select **Create a new security group**.

2. Type a name and description for your security group, or leave the default name and description. This new security group contains a rule that allows traffic to the ports that you configured your load balancer to use.

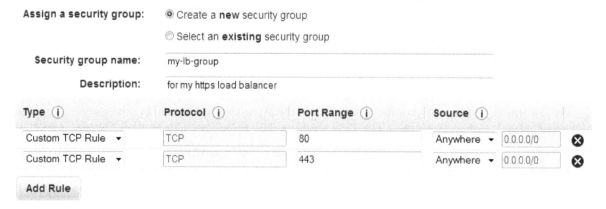

3. Choose **Next: Configure Security Settings**.

Step 3: Configure Security Settings

When you use HTTPS or SSL for your front-end listener, you must deploy an SSL certificate on your load balancer. The load balancer uses the certificate to terminate the connection and then decrypt requests from clients before sending them to the instances.

You must also specify a security policy. Elastic Load Balancing provides security policies that have predefined SSL negotiation configurations, or you can create your own custom security policy.

If you configured HTTPS/SSL on the back-end connection, you can enable authentication of your instances.

To configure security settings

1. For **Select Certificate**, do one of the following:

   - If you created or imported a certificate using AWS Certificate Manager, select **Choose an existing certificate from AWS Certificate Manager (ACM)**, and then select the certificate from **Certificate**.
   - If you imported a certificate using IAM, select **Choose an existing certificate from AWS Identity and Access Management (IAM)**, and then select your certificate from **Certificate**.
   - If you have a certificate to import but ACM is not available in your region, select **Upload a new SSL Certificate to AWS Identity and Access Management (IAM)**. Type the name of the certificate. In **Private Key**, copy and paste the contents of the private key file (PEM-encoded). In **Public Key Certificate**, copy and paste the contents of the public key certificate file (PEM-encoded). In **Certificate Chain**, copy and paste the contents of the certificate chain file (PEM-encoded), unless you are using a self-signed certificate and it's not important that browsers implicitly accept the certificate.

2. For **Select a Cipher**, verify that **Predefined Security Policy** is selected and set to **ELBSecurityPolicy-2016-08**. We recommend that you always use the latest predefined security policy. If you need to use a different predefined security policy or create a custom policy, see Update the SSL Negotiation Configuration.

3. (Optional) If you configured the HTTPS listener to communicate with instances using an encrypted connection, you can optionally set up authentication of the instances.

   1. For **Backend Certificate**, select **Enable backend authentication. Note**
      If you do not see the **Backend Certificate** section, go back to **Listener Configuration** and select **HTTPS (Secure HTTP)** for **Instance Protocol**.

   2. For **Certificate name**, type the name of the public key certificate.

   3. For **Certificate Body (pem encoded)**, copy and paste the contents of the certificate. The load balancer communicates with an instance only if its public key matches this key.

   4. To add another certificate, choose **Add another backend certificate**.

○ Proceed without backend authentication

◉ Enable backend authentication

Backend Certificate 1

Certificate Name   **Certificate Body (pem encoded)***

. . .

my-server-certificate

Add another backend certificate

4. Choose **Next: Configure Health Check**.

Step 4: Configure Health Checks

Elastic Load Balancing automatically checks the health of the registered EC2 instances for your load balancer. If Elastic Load Balancing finds an unhealthy instance, it stops sending traffic to the instance and reroutes traffic to the healthy instances. For more information about configuring health checks, see Configure Health Checks for Your Classic Load Balancer.

To configure health checks for your instances

1. On the **Configure Health Check** page, select a ping protocol and ping port. Your EC2 instances must accept the specified traffic on the specified ping port.

2. For **Ping Path**, replace the default value with a single forward slash (”/”). This tells Elastic Load Balancing to send health check requests to the default home page for your web server, such as `index.html`.

3. Keep the other settings at their default values.

4. Choose **Next: Add EC2 Instances**.

Step 5: Register EC2 Instances with Your Load Balancer

Your load balancer distributes traffic between the instances that are registered to it. You can select EC2 instances in a single Availability Zone or multiple Availability Zones within the same region as the load balancer. For more information, see Registered Instances for Your Classic Load Balancer.

Note
When you register an instance with an elastic network interface (ENI) attached, the load balancer routes traffic to the primary IP address of the primary interface (eth0) of the instance.

To register EC2 instances with your load balancer

1. On the **Add EC2 Instances** page, select the instances to register with your load balancer.

2. Leave cross-zone load balancing and connection draining enabled.

3. Choose **Next: Add Tags**.

Step 6: Tag Your Load Balancer (Optional)

You can tag your load balancer, or continue to the next step.

To add tags to your load balancer

1. On the **Add Tags** page, specify a key and a value for the tag.

2. To add another tag, choose **Create Tag** and specify a key and a value for the tag.

3. After you are finished adding tags, choose **Review and Create**.

Step 7: Create and Verify Your Load Balancer

Before you create the load balancer, review the settings that you selected. After creating the load balancer, you can verify that it's sending traffic to your EC2 instances.

To create and test your load balancer

1. On the **Review** page, check your settings. If you need to make changes, choose the corresponding link to edit the settings.

2. Choose **Create**.

3. After you are notified that your load balancer was created, choose **Close**.

4. Select your new load balancer.

5. On the **Description** tab, check the **Status** row. If it indicates that some of your instances are not in service, its probably because they are still in the registration process. For more information, see Troubleshoot a Classic Load Balancer: Instance Registration.

6. (Optional) After at least one of your EC2 instances is in service, you can test your load balancer. Copy the string from **DNS name** (for example, my-load-balancer-1234567890.us-west-2.elb.amazonaws.com) and paste it into the address field of an Internet-connected web browser. If your load balancer is working, you see the default page of your server.

Step 8: Delete Your Load Balancer (Optional)

As soon as your load balancer becomes available, you are billed for each hour or partial hour that you keep it running. When you no longer need a load balancer, you can delete it. As soon as the load balancer is deleted, you stop incurring charges for it.

To delete your load balancer

1. Open the Amazon EC2 console at https://console.aws.amazon.com/ec2/.

2. On the navigation pane, under **LOAD BALANCING**, choose **Load Balancers**.

3. Select the load balancer.

4. Choose **Actions, Delete**.

5. When prompted for confirmation, choose **Yes, Delete**.

6. (Optional) After you delete a load balancer, the EC2 instances associated with the load balancer continue to run, and you are billed for each hour or partial hour that you keep them running. For information about stopping or terminating your instances, see Stop and Start Your Instance or Terminate Your Instance in the *Amazon EC2 User Guide for Linux Instances*.

Create an HTTPS/SSL Load Balancer Using the AWS CLI

Use the following instructions to create an HTTPS/SSL load balancer using the AWS CLI.

Topics

- Step 1: Configure Listeners
- Step 2: Configure the SSL Security Policy
- Step 3: Configure Back-end Instance Authentication (Optional)
- Step 4: Configure Health Checks (Optional)
- Step 5: Register EC2 Instances
- Step 6: Verify the Instances
- Step 7: Delete Your Load Balancer (Optional)

Step 1: Configure Listeners

A *listener* is a process that checks for connection requests. It is configured with a protocol and a port for front-end (client to load balancer) connections and a protocol and port for back-end (load balancer to instance) connections. For information about the ports, protocols, and listener configurations supported by Elastic Load Balancing, see Listeners for Your Classic Load Balancer.

In this example, you configure two listeners for your load balancer by specifying the ports and protocols to use for front-end and back-end connections. The first listener accepts HTTP requests on port 80 and sends the requests to the instances on port 80 using HTTP. The second listener accepts HTTPS requests on port 443 and sends requests to instances using HTTP on port 80.

Because the second listener uses HTTPS for the front-end connection, you must deploy an SSL sever certificate on your load balancer. The load balancer uses the certificate to terminate and then decrypt requests before sending them to the instances.

To configure listeners for your load balancer

1. Get the Amazon Resource Name (ARN) of the SSL certificate. For example:

   ACM

   ```
   1 arn:aws:acm:region:123456789012:certificate/12345678-1234-1234-1234-123456789012
   ```

   IAM

   ```
   1 arn:aws:iam::123456789012:server-certificate/my-server-certificate
   ```

2. Use the following create-load-balancer command to configure the load balancer with the two listeners:

   ```
   1 aws elb create-load-balancer --load-balancer-name my-load-balancer --listeners "Protocol=
       http,LoadBalancerPort=80,InstanceProtocol=http,InstancePort=80" "Protocol=https,
       LoadBalancerPort=443,InstanceProtocol=http,InstancePort=80,SSLCertificateId="ARN" --
       availability-zones us-west-2a
   ```

   The following is an example response:

   ```
   1 {
   2   "DNSName": "my-loadbalancer-012345678.us-west-2.elb.amazonaws.com"
   3 }
   ```

3. (Optional) Use the following describe-load-balancers command to view the details of your load balancer:

```
1 aws elb describe-load-balancers --load-balancer-name my-load-balancer
```

Step 2: Configure the SSL Security Policy

You can select one of the predefined security policies, or you can create your own custom security policy. Otherwise, Elastic Load Balancing configures your load balancer with the default predefined security policy, ELBSecurityPolicy-2016-08. We recommend that you use the default security policy. For more information about security policies, see SSL Negotiation Configurations for Classic Load Balancers.

To verify that your load balancer is associated with the default security policy
Use the following describe-load-balancers command:

```
1 aws elb describe-load-balancers --load-balancer-name my-loadbalancer
```

The following is an example response. Note that ELBSecurityPolicy-2016-08 is associated with the load balancer on port 443.

```
1  {
2      "LoadBalancerDescriptions": [
3          {
4              ...
5              "ListenerDescriptions": [
6                  {
7                      "Listener": {
8                          "InstancePort": 80,
9                          "SSLCertificateId": "ARN",
10                         "LoadBalancerPort": 443,
11                         "Protocol": "HTTPS",
12                         "InstanceProtocol": "HTTP"
13                     },
14                     "PolicyNames": [
15                         "ELBSecurityPolicy-2016-08"
16                     ]
17                 },
18                 {
19                     "Listener": {
20                         "InstancePort": 80,
21                         "LoadBalancerPort": 80,
22                         "Protocol": "HTTP",
23                         "InstanceProtocol": "HTTP"
24                     },
25                     "PolicyNames": []
26                 }
27             ],
28             ...
29         }
30     ]
31 }
```

If you prefer, you can configure the SSL security policy for your load balancer instead of using the default security policy.

(Optional) To use a predefined SSL security policy

1. Use the following describe-load-balancer-policies command to list the names of the predefined security policies:

```
1 aws elb describe-load-balancer-policies
```

For information about the configuration for the predefined security policies, see Predefined SSL Security Policies.

2. Use the following create-load-balancer-policy command to create an SSL negotiation policy using one of the predefined security policies that you described in the previous step:

```
1 aws elb create-load-balancer-policy --load-balancer-name my-loadbalancer
2 --policy-name my-SSLNegotiation-policy --policy-type-name SSLNegotiationPolicyType
3 --policy-attributes AttributeName=Reference-Security-Policy,AttributeValue=predefined-
    policy
```

3. (Optional) Use the following describe-load-balancer-policies command to verify that the policy is created:

```
1 aws elb describe-load-balancer-policies --load-balancer-name my-loadbalancer --policy-name
    my-SSLNegotiation-policy
```

The response includes the description of the policy.

4. Use the following set-load-balancer-policies-of-listener command to enable the policy on load balancer port 443:

```
1 aws elb set-load-balancer-policies-of-listener --load-balancer-name my-loadbalancer --load-
    balancer-port 443 --policy-names my-SSLNegotiation-policy
```

Note
The `set-load-balancer-policies-of-listener` command replaces the current set of policies for the specified load balancer port with the specified set of policies. The `--policy-names` list must include all policies to be enabled. If you omit a policy that is currently enabled, it is disabled.

1. (Optional) Use the following describe-load-balancers command to verify that the policy is enabled:

```
1 aws elb describe-load-balancers --load-balancer-name my-loadbalancer
```

The following is an example response showing that the policy is enabled on port 443.

```
1  {
2      "LoadBalancerDescriptions": [
3          {
4              ....
5              "ListenerDescriptions": [
6                  {
7                      "Listener": {
8                          "InstancePort": 80,
9                          "SSLCertificateId": "ARN",
10                         "LoadBalancerPort": 443,
11                         "Protocol": "HTTPS",
12                         "InstanceProtocol": "HTTP"
13                     },
14                     "PolicyNames": [
15                         "my-SSLNegotiation-policy"
16                     ]
17                 },
18                 {
19                     "Listener": {
```

```
20              "InstancePort": 80,
21              "LoadBalancerPort": 80,
22              "Protocol": "HTTP",
23              "InstanceProtocol": "HTTP"
24            },
25            "PolicyNames": []
26          }
27        ],
28        ...
29      }
30    ]
31 }
```

When you create a custom security policy, you must enable at least one protocol and one cipher. The DSA and RSA ciphers are specific to the signing algorithm and are used to create the SSL certificate. If you already have your SSL certificate, make sure to enable the cipher that was used to create your certificate. The name of your custom policy must not begin with ELBSecurityPolicy- or ELBSample-, as these prefixes are reserved for the names of the predefined security policies.

(Optional) To use a custom SSL security policy

1. Use the create-load-balancer-policy command to create an SSL negotiation policy using a custom security policy. For example:

```
1 aws elb create-load-balancer-policy --load-balancer-name my-loadbalancer
2  --policy-name my-SSLNegotiation-policy --policy-type-name SSLNegotiationPolicyType
3  --policy-attributes AttributeName=Protocol-TLSv1.2,AttributeValue=true
4  AttributeName=Protocol-TLSv1.1,AttributeValue=true
5  AttributeName=DHE-RSA-AES256-SHA256,AttributeValue=true
6  AttributeName=Server-Defined-Cipher-Order,AttributeValue=true
```

2. (Optional) Use the following describe-load-balancer-policies command to verify that the policy is created:

```
1 aws elb describe-load-balancer-policies --load-balancer-name my-loadbalancer --policy-name
    my-SSLNegotiation-policy
```

The response includes the description of the policy.

3. Use the following set-load-balancer-policies-of-listener command to enable the policy on load balancer port 443:

```
1 aws elb set-load-balancer-policies-of-listener --load-balancer-name my-loadbalancer --load-
    balancer-port 443 --policy-names my-SSLNegotiation-policy
```

Note
The set-load-balancer-policies-of-listener command replaces the current set of policies for the specified load balancer port with the specified set of policies. The --policy-names list must include all policies to be enabled. If you omit a policy that is currently enabled, it is disabled.

1. (Optional) Use the following describe-load-balancers command to verify that the policy is enabled:

```
1 aws elb describe-load-balancers --load-balancer-name my-loadbalancer
```

The following is an example response showing that the policy is enabled on port 443.

```
1 {
2     "LoadBalancerDescriptions": [
3         {
4             ....
```

```
 5          "ListenerDescriptions": [
 6              {
 7                  "Listener": {
 8                      "InstancePort": 80,
 9                      "SSLCertificateId": "ARN",
10                      "LoadBalancerPort": 443,
11                      "Protocol": "HTTPS",
12                      "InstanceProtocol": "HTTP"
13                  },
14                  "PolicyNames": [
15                      "my-SSLNegotiation-policy"
16                  ]
17              },
18              {
19                  "Listener": {
20                      "InstancePort": 80,
21                      "LoadBalancerPort": 80,
22                      "Protocol": "HTTP",
23                      "InstanceProtocol": "HTTP"
24                  },
25                  "PolicyNames": []
26              }
27          ],
28          ...
29      }
30  ]
31 }
```

Step 3: Configure Back-end Instance Authentication (Optional)

If you set up HTTPS/SSL on the back-end connection, you can optionally set up authentication of your instances.

When you set up back-end instance authentication, you create a public key policy. Next, you use this public key policy to create a back-end instance authentication policy. Finally, you set the back-end instance authentication policy with the instance port for the HTTPS protocol.

The load balancer communicates with an instance only if the public key that the instance presents to the load balancer matches a public key in the authentication policy for your load balancer.

To configure back-end instance authentication

1. Use the following command to retrieve the public key:

```
1 openssl x509 -in your X509 certificate PublicKey -pubkey -noout
```

2. Use the following create-load-balancer-policy command to create a public key policy:

```
1 aws elb create-load-balancer-policy --load-balancer-name my-loadbalancer --policy-name my-
      PublicKey-policy \
2 --policy-type-name PublicKeyPolicyType --policy-attributes AttributeName=PublicKey,
      AttributeValue=MIICiTCCAfICCQD6m7oRw0uXOjANBgkqhkiG9w
3 0BAQUFADCBiDELMAkGA1UEBhMCVVMxCzAJBgNVBAgTAldBMRAwDgYDVQQHEwdTZ
4 WF0dGxlMQ8wDQYDVQQKEwZBbWF6b24xFDASBgNVBAsTC0lBTSBDb25zb2xlMRIw
5 EAYDVQQDEwlUZXN0Q2lsYWMxHzAdBgkqhkiG9w0BCQEWEG5vb251QGFtYXpvbi5
6 jb20wHhcNMTEwNDI1MjA0NTIxWhcNMTIwNDI0MjA0NTIxWjCBiDELMAkGA1UEBh
7 MCVVMxCzAJBgNVBAgTAldBMRAwDgYDVQQHEwdTZWF0dGxlMQ8wDQYDVQQKEwZBb
8 WF6b24xFDASBgNVBAsTC0lBTSBDb25zb2xlMRIwEAYDVQQDEwlUZXN0Q2lsYWMx
```

```
 9   HzAdBgkqhkiG9wOBCQEWEG5vb251QGFtYXpvbi5jb20wgZ8wDQYJKoZIhvcNAQE
10   BBQADgYOAMIGJAoGBAMaKOdn+a4GmWIWJ21uUSfwfEvySWtC2XADZ4nB+BLYgVI
11   k60CpiwsZ3G93vUEIO3IyNoH/fOwYK8m9TrDHudUZg3qX4waLG5M43q7Wgc/MbQ
12   ITxOUSQv7c7ugFFDzQGBzZswY6786m86gpEIbb3OhjZnzcvQAaRHhd1QWIMm2nr
13   AgMBAAEwDQYJKoZIhvcNAQEFBQADgYEAtCu4nUhVVxYUntneD9+h8Mg9q6q+auN
14   KyExzyLwaxlAoo7TJHidbtS4J5iNmZgXLOFkbFFBjvSfpJIlJOOzbhNYS5f6Guo
15   EDmFJlOZxBHjJnyp378OD8uTs7fLvjx79LjSTbNYiytVbZPQUQ5Yaxu2jXnimvw
16   3rrszlaEXAMPLE=
```

Note

To specify a public key value for --policy-attributes, remove the first and last lines of the public key (the line containing "-----BEGIN PUBLIC KEY-----" and the line containing "-----END PUBLIC KEY-----"). The AWS CLI does not accept white space characters in --policy-attributes.

1. Use the following create-load-balancer-policy command to create a back-end instance authentication policy using my-PublicKey-policy.

```
1 aws elb create-load-balancer-policy --load-balancer-name my-loadbalancer --policy-name my-
    authentication-policy --policy-type-name BackendServerAuthenticationPolicyType --policy
    -attributes AttributeName=PublicKeyPolicyName,AttributeValue=my-PublicKey-policy
```

You can optionally use multiple public key policies. The load balancer tries all the keys, one at a time. If the public key presented by an instance matches one of these public keys, the instance is authenticated.

2. Use the following set-load-balancer-policies-for-backend-server command to set my-authentication-policy to the instance port for HTTPS. In this example, the instance port is port 443.

```
1 aws elb set-load-balancer-policies-for-backend-server --load-balancer-name my-loadbalancer
    --instance-port 443 --policy-names my-authentication-policy
```

3. (Optional) Use the following describe-load-balancer-policies command to list all the policies for your load balancer:

```
1 aws elb describe-load-balancer-policies --load-balancer-name my-loadbalancer
```

4. (Optional) Use the following describe-load-balancer-policies command to view details of the policy:

```
1 aws elb describe-load-balancer-policies --load-balancer-name my-loadbalancer --policy-names
    my-authentication-policy
```

Step 4: Configure Health Checks (Optional)

Elastic Load Balancing regularly checks the health of each registered EC2 instance based on the health checks that you configured. If Elastic Load Balancing finds an unhealthy instance, it stops sending traffic to the instance and routes traffic to the healthy instances. For more information, see Configure Health Checks for Your Classic Load Balancer.

When you create your load balancer, Elastic Load Balancing uses default settings for the health checks. If you prefer, you can change the health check configuration for your load balancer instead of using the default settings.

To configure the health checks for your instances

Use the following configure-health-check command:

```
1 aws elb configure-health-check --load-balancer-name my-loadbalancer --health-check Target=HTTP
    :80/ping,Interval=30,UnhealthyThreshold=2,HealthyThreshold=2,Timeout=3
```

The following is an example response:

```
1  {
2      "HealthCheck": {
3          "HealthyThreshold": 2,
4          "Interval": 30,
5          "Target": "HTTP:80/ping",
6          "Timeout": 3,
7          "UnhealthyThreshold": 2
8      }
9  }
```

Step 5: Register EC2 Instances

After you create your load balancer, you must register your EC2 instances with the load balancer. You can select EC2 instances from a single Availability Zone or multiple Availability Zones within the same region as the load balancer. For more information, see Registered Instances for Your Classic Load Balancer.

Use the register-instances-with-load-balancer command as follows:

```
1  aws elb register-instances-with-load-balancer --load-balancer-name my-loadbalancer --instances i
     -4f8cf126 i-0bb7ca62
```

The following is an example response:

```
1  {
2      "Instances": [
3          {
4              "InstanceId": "i-4f8cf126"
5          },
6          {
7              "InstanceId": "i-0bb7ca62"
8          }
9      ]
10 }
```

Step 6: Verify the Instances

Your load balancer is usable as soon as any one of your registered instances is in the InService state.

To check the state of your newly registered EC2 instances, use the following describe-instance-health command:

```
1  aws elb describe-instance-health  --load-balancer-name my-loadbalancer --instances i-4f8cf126 i
     -0bb7ca62
```

The following is an example response:

```
1  {
2      "InstanceStates": [
3          {
4              "InstanceId": "i-4f8cf126",
5              "ReasonCode": "N/A",
6              "State": "InService",
7              "Description": "N/A"
8          },
9          {
10             "InstanceId": "i-0bb7ca62",
```

```
11          "ReasonCode": "Instance",
12          "State": "OutOfService",
13          "Description": "Instance registration is still in progress"
14      }
15    ]
16 }
```

If the `State` field for an instance is `OutOfService`, it's probably because your instances are still registering. For more information, see Troubleshoot a Classic Load Balancer: Instance Registration.

After the state of at least one of your instances is `InService`, you can test your load balancer. To test your load balancer, copy the DNS name of the load balancer and paste it into the address field of an Internet-connected web browser. If your load balancer is working, you see the default page of your HTTP server.

Step 7: Delete Your Load Balancer (Optional)

Deleting a the load balancer automatically de-registers its associated EC2 instances. As soon as the load balancer is deleted, you stop incurring charges for that load balancer. However, the EC2 instances continue run and you continue to incur charges.

To delete your load balancer, use the following delete-load-balancer command:

```
1 aws elb delete-load-balancer --load-balancer-name my-loadbalancer
```

To stop your EC2 instances, use the stop-instances command. To terminate your EC2 instances, use the terminate-instances command.

Configure an HTTPS Listener for Your Classic Load Balancer

A *listener* is a process that checks for connection requests. It is configured with a protocol and a port for front-end (client to load balancer) connections and a protocol and a port for back-end (load balancer to instance) connections. For information about the ports, protocols, and listener configurations supported by Elastic Load Balancing, see Listeners for Your Classic Load Balancer.

If you have a load balancer with a listener that accepts HTTP requests on port 80, you can add a listener that accepts HTTPS requests on port 443. If you specify that the HTTPS listener sends requests to the instances on port 80, the load balancer terminates the SSL requests and communication from the load balancer to the instances is not encrypted. If the HTTPS listener sends requests to the instances on port 443, communication from the load balancer to the instances is encrypted.

If your load balancer uses an encrypted connection to communicate with instances, you can optionally enable authentication of the instances. This ensures that the load balancer communicates with an instance only if its public key matches the key that you specified to the load balancer for this purpose.

For information about creating a new HTTPS listener, see Create a Classic Load Balancer with an HTTPS Listener.

Topics

- Prerequisites
- Add an HTTPS Listener Using the Console
- Add an HTTPS Listener Using the AWS CLI

Prerequisites

To enable HTTPS support for an HTTPS listener, you must deploy an SSL server certificate on your load balancer. The load balancer uses the certificate to terminate and then decrypt requests before sending them to the instances. If you do not have an SSL certificate, you can create one. For more information, see SSL/TLS Certificates for Classic Load Balancers.

Add an HTTPS Listener Using the Console

You can add an HTTPS listener to an existing load balancer.

To add an HTTPS listener to your load balancer

1. Open the Amazon EC2 console at https://console.aws.amazon.com/ec2/.

2. On the navigation pane, under **LOAD BALANCING**, choose **Load Balancers**.

3. Select your load balancer.

4. On the **Listeners** tab, choose **Edit**.

5. On the **Edit listeners** page, choose **Add**.

6. For **Load Balancer Protocol**, select **HTTPS (Secure HTTP)**. This updates **Load Balancer Port**, **Instance Protocol**, and **Instance Port**. **Important**
   By default, the instance protocol is HTTP. If you want to set up back-end instance authentication, change the instance protocol to HTTPS (Secure HTTP). This also updates the instance port.

7. For **Cipher**, choose **Change**. Verify that **Predefined Security Policy** is selected and set to **ELBSecurityPolicy-2016-08**. We recommend that you always use the latest predefined security policy. If you need to use a different predefined security policy or create a custom policy, see Update the SSL Negotiation Configuration.

8. If you already have a certificate deployed on your load balancer and want to continue using it, you can skip this step.

   For **SSL Certificate**, choose **Change**, and then do one of the following:

   - If you create or imported a certificate using AWS Certificate Manager, select **Choose an existing certificate from AWS Certificate Manager (ACM)**, select the certificate from **Certificate**, and then choose **Save**. **Note**
     This option is available only in regions that support AWS Certificate Manager.
   - If you imported a certificate using IAM, select **Choose an existing certificate from AWS Identity and Access Management (IAM)**, select the certificate from **Certificate**, and then choose **Save**.
   - If you have an SSL certificate to import but ACM is not supported in this region, select **Upload a new SSL Certificate to AWS Identity and Access Management (IAM)**. Type the name of the certificate. In **Private Key**, copy and paste the contents of the private key file (PEM-encoded). In **Public Key Certificate**, copy and paste the contents of the public key certificate file (PEM-encoded). In **Certificate Chain**, copy and paste the contents of the certificate chain file (PEM-encoded), unless you are using a self-signed certificate and it's not important that browsers implicitly accept the certificate.

9. (Optional) Choose **Add** to add additional listeners.

10. Choose **Save** to add the listeners you just configured.

11. (Optional) To set up back-end instance authentication for an existing load balancer, you must use the AWS CLI or an API, as this task is not supported using the console. For more information, see Configure Back-end Instance Authentication.

Add an HTTPS Listener Using the AWS CLI

You can add an HTTPS listener to an existing load balancer.

To add an HTTPS listener to your load balancer using the AWS CLI

1. Get the Amazon Resource Name (ARN) of the SSL certificate. For example:

   ACM

   ```
   1 arn:aws:acm:region:123456789012:certificate/12345678-1234-1234-1234-123456789012
   ```

   IAM

   ```
   1 arn:aws:iam::123456789012:server-certificate/my-server-certificate
   ```

2. Use the following create-load-balancer-listeners command to add a listener to your load balancer that accepts HTTPS requests on port 443 and sends the requests to the instances on port 80 using HTTP:

   ```
   1 aws elb create-load-balancer-listeners --load-balancer-name my-load-balancer --listeners
       Protocol=HTTPS,LoadBalancerPort=443,InstanceProtocol=HTTP,InstancePort=80,
       SSLCertificateId=ARN
   ```

   If you want to set up back-end instance authentication, use the following command to add a listener that accepts HTTPS requests on port 443 and sends the requests to the instances on port 443 using HTTPS:

   ```
   1 aws elb create-load-balancer-listeners --load-balancer-name my-load-balancer --listeners
       Protocol=HTTPS,LoadBalancerPort=443,InstanceProtocol=HTTPS,InstancePort=443,
       SSLCertificateId=ARN
   ```

3. (Optional) You can use the following describe-load-balancers command to view the updated details of your load balancer:

   ```
   1 aws elb describe-load-balancers --load-balancer-name my-load-balancer
   ```

The following is an example response:

```
1  {
2      "LoadBalancerDescriptions": [
3          {
4              ...
5              "ListenerDescriptions": [
6                  {
7                      "Listener": {
8                          "InstancePort": 80,
9                          "SSLCertificateId": "ARN",
10                         "LoadBalancerPort": 443,
11                         "Protocol": "HTTPS",
12                         "InstanceProtocol": "HTTP"
13                     },
14                     "PolicyNames": [
15                         "ELBSecurityPolicy-2016-08"
16                     ]
17                 },
18                 {
19                     "Listener": {
20                         "InstancePort": 80,
21                         "LoadBalancerPort": 80,
22                         "Protocol": "HTTP",
23                         "InstanceProtocol": "HTTP"
24                     },
25                     "PolicyNames": []
26                 }
27             ],
28             ...
29         }
30     ]
31 }
```

4. (Optional) Your HTTPS listener was created using the default security policy. If you want to specify a different predefined security policy or a custom security policy, use the create-load-balancer-policy and set-load-balancer-policies-of-listener commands. For more information, see Update the SSL Negotiation Configuration Using the AWS CLI.

5. (Optional) To set up back-end instance authentication, use the set-load-balancer-policies-for-backend-server command. For more information, see Configure Back-end Instance Authentication.

Replace the SSL Certificate for Your Classic Load Balancer

If you have an HTTPS listener, you deployed an SSL server certificate on your load balancer when you created the listener. Each certificate comes with a validity period. You must ensure that you renew or replace the certificate before its validity period ends.

Certificates provided by AWS Certificate Manager and deployed on your load balancer can be renewed automatically. ACM attempts to renew certificates before they expire. For more information, see Managed Renewal in the *AWS Certificate Manager User Guide*. If you imported a certificate into ACM, you must monitor the expiration date of the certificate and renew it before it expires. For more information, see Importing Certificates in the *AWS Certificate Manager User Guide*. After a certificate that is deployed on a load balancer is renewed, new requests use the renewed certificate.

To replace a certificate, you must first create a new certificate by following the same steps that you used when you created the current certificate. Then, you can replace the certificate. After a certificate that is deployed on a load balancer is replaced, new requests use the new certificate.

Note that renewing or replacing a certificate does not affect requests that were already received by a load balancer node and are pending routing to a healthy target.

Topics

- Replace the SSL Certificate Using the Console
- Replace the SSL Certificate Using the AWS CLI

Replace the SSL Certificate Using the Console

You can replace the certificate deployed on your load balancer with a certificate provided by ACM or a certificate uploaded to IAM.

To replace the SSL certificate for an HTTPS load balancer

1. Open the Amazon EC2 console at https://console.aws.amazon.com/ec2/.

2. On the navigation pane, under **LOAD BALANCING**, choose **Load Balancers**.

3. Select your load balancer.

4. On the **Listeners** tab, for **SSL Certificate**, choose **Change**.

5. On the **Select Certificate** page, do one of the following:

   - If you created or imported a certificate using AWS Certificate Manager, select **Choose an existing certificate from AWS Certificate Manager (ACM)**, select the certificate from **Certificate**, and then choose **Save**.
   - If you imported a certificate using IAM, select **Choose an existing certificate from AWS Identity and Access Management (IAM)**, select the certificate from **Certificate**, and then choose **Save**.
   - If you have a certificate to import but ACM is not supported in the region, select **Upload a new SSL Certificate to AWS Identity and Access Management (IAM)**. Type a name for the certificate, copy the required information to the form, and then choose **Save**. Note that the certificate chain is not required if the certificate is a self-signed certificate.

Replace the SSL Certificate Using the AWS CLI

You can replace the certificate deployed on your load balancer with a certificate provided by ACM or a certificate uploaded to IAM.

To replace an SSL certificate with a certificate provided by ACM

1. Use the following request-certificate command to request a new certificate:

```
1 aws acm request-certificate --domain-name www.example.com
```

2. Use the following set-load-balancer-listener-ssl-certificate command to set the certificate:

```
1 aws elb set-load-balancer-listener-ssl-certificate --load-balancer-name my-load-balancer --
    load-balancer-port 443 --ssl-certificate-id arn:aws:acm:region:123456789012:certificate
    /12345678-1234-1234-1234-123456789012
```

To replace an SSL certificate with a certificate uploaded to IAM

1. If you have an SSL certificate but have not uploaded it, see Uploading a Server Certificate in the *IAM User Guide*.

2. Use the following get-server-certificate command to get the ARN of the certificate:

```
1 aws iam get-server-certificate --server-certificate-name my-new-certificate
```

3. Use the following set-load-balancer-listener-ssl-certificate command to set the certificate:

```
1 aws elb set-load-balancer-listener-ssl-certificate --load-balancer-name my-load-balancer --
    load-balancer-port 443 --ssl-certificate-id arn:aws:iam::123456789012:server-
    certificate/my-new-certificate
```

Update the SSL Negotiation Configuration of Your Classic Load Balancer

Elastic Load Balancing provides security policies that have predefined SSL negotiation configurations to use to negotiate SSL connections between clients and your load balancer. If you are using the HTTPS/SSL protocol for your listener, you can use one of the predefined security policies, or use your own custom security policy.

For more information about the security policies, see SSL Negotiation Configurations for Classic Load Balancers. For information about the configurations of the security policies provided by Elastic Load Balancing, see Predefined SSL Security Policies.

If you create an HTTPS/SSL listener without associating a security policy, Elastic Load Balancing associates the default predefined security policy, `ELBSecurityPolicy-2016-08`, with your load balancer.

If you have an existing load balancer with an SSL negotiation configuration that does not use the latest protocols and ciphers, we recommend that you update your load balancer to use ELBSecurityPolicy-2016-08. If you prefer, you can create a custom configuration. We strongly recommend that you test the new security policies before you upgrade your load balancer configuration.

The following examples show you how to update the SSL negotiation configuration for an HTTPS/SSL listener. Note that the change does not affect requests that were received by a load balancer node and are pending routing to a healthy instance, but the updated configuration will be used with new requests that are received.

Topics

- Update the SSL Negotiation Configuration Using the Console
- Update the SSL Negotiation Configuration Using the AWS CLI

Update the SSL Negotiation Configuration Using the Console

By default, Elastic Load Balancing associates the latest predefined policy with your load balancer. When a new predefined policy is added, we recommend that you update your load balancer to use the new predefined policy. Alternatively, you can select a different predefined security policy or create a custom policy.

To update SSL negotiation configuration for an HTTPS/SSL load balancer

1. Open the Amazon EC2 console at https://console.aws.amazon.com/ec2/.

2. On the navigation pane, under **LOAD BALANCING**, choose **Load Balancers**.

3. Select your load balancer.

4. On the **Listeners** tab, for **Cipher**, choose **Change**.

5. On the **Select a Cipher** page, select a security policy using one of the following options:

   - (Recommended) Select **Predefined Security Policy**, keep the default policy, **ELBSecurityPolicy-2016-08**, and then choose **Save**.

   - Select **Predefined Security Policy**, select a predefined policy other than the default, and then choose **Save**.

   - Select **Custom Security Policy** and enable at least one protocol and one cipher as follows:

     1. For **SSL Protocols**, select one or more protocols to enable.

     2. For **SSL Options**, select **Server Order Preference** to use the order listed in the Predefined SSL Security Policies for SSL negotiation.

3. For **SSL Ciphers**, select one or more ciphers to enable. If you already have an SSL certificate, you must enable the cipher that was used to create the certificate, because DSA and RSA ciphers are specific to the signing algorithm.

4. Choose **Save**.

Update the SSL Negotiation Configuration Using the AWS CLI

You can use the default predefined security policy, ELBSecurityPolicy-2016-08, a different predefined security policy, or a custom security policy.

To use a predefined SSL security policy

1. Use the following describe-load-balancer-policies command to list the predefined security policies provided by Elastic Load Balancing:

```
1 aws elb describe-load-balancer-policies --query "PolicyDescriptions[?PolicyTypeName==`
    SSLNegotiationPolicyType`].{PolicyName:PolicyName}" --output table
```

The following is example output:

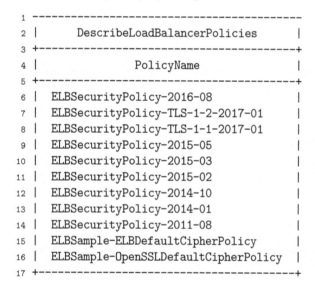

```
1 --------------------------------------------
2 |          DescribeLoadBalancerPolicies      |
3 +------------------------------------------+
4 |                 PolicyName                 |
5 +------------------------------------------+
6 |  ELBSecurityPolicy-2016-08                 |
7 |  ELBSecurityPolicy-TLS-1-2-2017-01         |
8 |  ELBSecurityPolicy-TLS-1-1-2017-01         |
9 |  ELBSecurityPolicy-2015-05                 |
10 |  ELBSecurityPolicy-2015-03                 |
11 |  ELBSecurityPolicy-2015-02                 |
12 |  ELBSecurityPolicy-2014-10                 |
13 |  ELBSecurityPolicy-2014-01                 |
14 |  ELBSecurityPolicy-2011-08                 |
15 |  ELBSample-ELBDefaultCipherPolicy          |
16 |  ELBSample-OpenSSLDefaultCipherPolicy      |
17 +------------------------------------------+
```

To determine which ciphers are enabled for a policy, use the following command:

```
1 aws elb describe-load-balancer-policies --policy-names ELBSecurityPolicy-2016-08 --output
    table
```

For information about the configuration for the predefined security policies, see Predefined SSL Security Policies.

2. Use the create-load-balancer-policy command to create an SSL negotiation policy using one of the predefined security policies that you described in the previous step. For example, the following command uses the default predefined security policy:

```
1 aws elb create-load-balancer-policy --load-balancer-name my-loadbalancer
2 --policy-name my-SSLNegotiation-policy  --policy-type-name SSLNegotiationPolicyType
3 --policy-attributes AttributeName=Reference-Security-Policy,AttributeValue=
    ELBSecurityPolicy-2016-08
```

If you exceed the limit on the number of policies for the load balancer, use the delete-load-balancer-policy command to delete any unused policies.

3. (Optional) Use the following describe-load-balancer-policies command to verify that the policy is created:

```
1 aws elb describe-load-balancer-policies --load-balancer-name my-loadbalancer --policy-name
    my-SSLNegotiation-policy
```

The response includes the description of the policy.

4. Use the following set-load-balancer-policies-of-listener command to enable the policy on load balancer port 443:

```
1 aws elb set-load-balancer-policies-of-listener --load-balancer-name my-loadbalancer --load-
    balancer-port 443 --policy-names my-SSLNegotiation-policy
```

Note

The `set-load-balancer-policies-of-listener` command replaces the current set of policies for the specified load balancer port with the the specified set of policies. The `--policy-names` list must include all policies to be enabled. If you omit a policy that is currently enabled, it is disabled.

1. (Optional) Use the following describe-load-balancers command to verify that the new policy is enabled for the load balancer port:

```
1 aws elb describe-load-balancers --load-balancer-name my-loadbalancer
```

The response shows that the policy is enabled on port 443.

```
1  ...
2  {
3      "Listener": {
4          "InstancePort": 443,
5          "SSLCertificateId": "ARN",
6          "LoadBalancerPort": 443,
7          "Protocol": "HTTPS",
8          "InstanceProtocol": "HTTPS"
9      },
10     "PolicyNames": [
11         "my-SSLNegotiation-policy"
12     ]
13 }
14 ...
```

When you create a custom security policy, you must enable at least one protocol and one cipher. The DSA and RSA ciphers are specific to the signing algorithm and are used to create the SSL certificate. If you already have an SSL certificate, be sure to enable the cipher that was used to create the certificate. The name of your custom policy must not begin with `ELBSecurityPolicy-` or `ELBSample-`, as these prefixes are reserved for the names of the predefined security policies.

To use a custom SSL security policy

1. Use the create-load-balancer-policy command to create an SSL negotiation policy using a custom security policy. For example:

```
1 aws elb create-load-balancer-policy --load-balancer-name my-loadbalancer
2 --policy-name my-SSLNegotiation-policy --policy-type-name SSLNegotiationPolicyType
3 --policy-attributes AttributeName=Protocol-TLSv1.2,AttributeValue=true
4 AttributeName=Protocol-TLSv1.1,AttributeValue=true
5 AttributeName=DHE-RSA-AES256-SHA256,AttributeValue=true
6 AttributeName=Server-Defined-Cipher-Order,AttributeValue=true
```

If you exceed the limit on the number of policies for the load balancer, use the delete-load-balancer-policy command to delete any unused policies.

2. (Optional) Use the following describe-load-balancer-policies command to verify that the policy is created:

```
1 aws elb describe-load-balancer-policies --load-balancer-name my-loadbalancer --policy-name
     my-SSLNegotiation-policy
```

The response includes the description of the policy.

3. Use the following set-load-balancer-policies-of-listener command to enable the policy on load balancer port 443:

```
1 aws elb set-load-balancer-policies-of-listener --load-balancer-name my-loadbalancer --load-
     balancer-port 443 --policy-names my-SSLNegotiation-policy
```

Note

The `set-load-balancer-policies-of-listener` command replaces the current set of policies for the specified load balancer port with the the specified set of policies. The `--policy-names` list must include all policies to be enabled. If you omit a policy that is currently enabled, it is disabled.

1. (Optional) Use the following describe-load-balancers command to verify that the new policy is enabled for the load balancer port:

```
1 aws elb describe-load-balancers --load-balancer-name my-loadbalancer
```

The response shows that the policy is enabled on port 443.

```
1  ...
2  {
3      "Listener": {
4          "InstancePort": 443,
5          "SSLCertificateId": "ARN",
6          "LoadBalancerPort": 443,
7          "Protocol": "HTTPS",
8          "InstanceProtocol": "HTTPS"
9      },
10     "PolicyNames": [
11         "my-SSLNegotiation-policy"
12     ]
13 }
14 ...
```

Configure Your Classic Load Balancer

Topics

- Configure the Idle Connection Timeout for Your Classic Load Balancer
- Configure Cross-Zone Load Balancing for Your Classic Load Balancer
- Configure Connection Draining for Your Classic Load Balancer
- Configure Proxy Protocol Support for Your Classic Load Balancer
- Configure Sticky Sessions for Your Classic Load Balancer
- Tag Your Classic Load Balancer
- Configure a Custom Domain Name for Your Classic Load Balancer

Configure the Idle Connection Timeout for Your Classic Load Balancer

For each request that a client makes through a Classic Load Balancer, the load balancer maintains two connections. One connection is with the client and the other connection is with a registered EC2 instance. For each connection, the load balancer manages an idle timeout that is triggered when no data is sent over the connection for a specified time period. If no data has been sent or received by the time that the idle timeout period elapses, the load balancer closes the connection.

By default, Elastic Load Balancing sets the idle timeout to 60 seconds for both connections. Therefore, if the instance doesn't send some data at least every 60 seconds while the request is in flight, the load balancer can close the connection. To ensure that lengthy operations such as file uploads have time to complete, send at least 1 byte of data before each idle timeout period elapses, and increase the length of the idle timeout period as needed.

If you use HTTP and HTTPS listeners, we recommend that you enable the HTTP keep-alive option for your instances. You can enable keep-alive in your web server settings or in the kernel settings for your instances. Keep-alive, when enabled, enables the load balancer to reuse connections to your instance, which reduces the CPU utilization. To ensure that the load balancer is responsible for closing the connections to your instance, make sure that the value you set for the HTTP keep-alive time is greater than the idle timeout setting on your load balancer.

Note that TCP keep-alive probes do not prevent the load balancer from terminating the connection because they do not send data in the payload.

Topics

- Configure the Idle Timeout Using the Console
- Configure the Idle Timeout Using the AWS CLI

Configure the Idle Timeout Using the Console

Use the following procedure to set the idle timeout for your load balancer.

To configure the idle timeout setting for your load balancer

1. Open the Amazon EC2 console at https://console.aws.amazon.com/ec2/.

2. On the navigation pane, under **LOAD BALANCING**, choose **Load Balancers**.

3. Select your load balancer.

4. On the **Description** tab, choose **Edit idle timeout**.

5. On the **Configure Connection Settings** page, type a value for **Idle timeout**. The range for the idle timeout is from 1 to 4,000 seconds.

6. Choose **Save**.

Configure the Idle Timeout Using the AWS CLI

Use the following modify-load-balancer-attributes command to set the idle timeout for your load balancer:

```
1  aws elb modify-load-balancer-attributes --load-balancer-name my-loadbalancer --load-balancer-
       attributes "{\"ConnectionSettings\":{\"IdleTimeout\":30}}"
```

The following is an example response:

```json
1  {
2      "LoadBalancerAttributes": {
3          "ConnectionSettings": {
4              "IdleTimeout": 30
5          }
6      },
7      "LoadBalancerName": "my-loadbalancer"
8  }
```

Configure Cross-Zone Load Balancing for Your Classic Load Balancer

With *cross-zone load balancing*, each load balancer node for your Classic Load Balancer distributes requests evenly across the registered instances in all enabled Availability Zones. If cross-zone load balancing is disabled, each load balancer node distributes requests evenly across the registered instances in its Availability Zone only. For more information, see Cross-Zone Load Balancing in the *Elastic Load Balancing User Guide*.

Cross-zone load balancing reduces the need to maintain equivalent numbers of instances in each enabled Availability Zone, and improves your application's ability to handle the loss of one or more instances. However, we still recommend that you maintain approximately equivalent numbers of instances in each enabled Availability Zone for higher fault tolerance.

For environments where clients cache DNS lookups, incoming requests might favor one of the Availability Zones. Using cross-zone load balancing, this imbalance in the request load is spread across all available instances in the region, reducing the impact of misbehaving clients.

When you create a Classic Load Balancer, the default for cross-zone load balancing depends on how you create the load balancer. With the API or CLI, cross-zone load balancing is disabled by default. With the AWS Management Console, the option to enable cross-zone load balancing is selected by default. After you create a Classic Load Balancer, you can enable or disable cross-zone load balancing at any time.

Topics

- Enable Cross-Zone Load Balancing
- Disable Cross-Zone Load Balancing

Enable Cross-Zone Load Balancing

You can enable cross-zone load balancing for your Classic Load Balancer at any time.

To enable cross-zone load balancing using the console

1. Open the Amazon EC2 console at https://console.aws.amazon.com/ec2/.

2. On the navigation pane, under **LOAD BALANCING**, choose **Load Balancers**.

3. Select your load balancer.

4. On the **Description** tab, choose **Change cross-zone load balancing setting**.

5. On the **Configure Cross-Zone Load Balancing** page, select **Enable**.

6. Choose **Save**.

To enable cross-zone load balancing using the AWS CLI

1. Use the following modify-load-balancer-attributes command to set the `CrossZoneLoadBalancing` attribute of your load balancer to `true`:

```
1 aws elb modify-load-balancer-attributes --load-balancer-name my-loadbalancer --load-
      balancer-attributes "{\"CrossZoneLoadBalancing\":{\"Enabled\":true}}"
```

The following is an example response:

```
1 {
2     "LoadBalancerAttributes": {
3       "CrossZoneLoadBalancing": {
4           "Enabled": true
5         }
6     },
7     "LoadBalancerName": "my-loadbalancer"
```

```
8  }
```

2. (Optional) Use the following describe-load-balancer-attributes command to verify that cross-zone load balancing is enabled for your load balancer:

```
1 aws elb describe-load-balancer-attributes --load-balancer-name my-loadbalancer
```

The following is an example response:

```
1  {
2      "LoadBalancerAttributes": {
3          "ConnectionDraining": {
4              "Enabled": false,
5              "Timeout": 300
6          },
7          "CrossZoneLoadBalancing": {
8              "Enabled": true
9          },
10         "ConnectionSettings": {
11             "IdleTimeout": 60
12         },
13         "AccessLog": {
14             "Enabled": false
15         }
16     }
17 }
```

Disable Cross-Zone Load Balancing

You can disable the cross-zone load balancing option for your load balancer at any time.

To disable cross-zone load balancing using the console

1. Open the Amazon EC2 console at https://console.aws.amazon.com/ec2/.

2. On the navigation pane, under **LOAD BALANCING**, choose **Load Balancers**.

3. Select your load balancer.

4. On the **Description** tab, choose **Change cross-zone load balancing**.

5. On the **Configure Cross-Zone Load Balancing** page, select **Disable**.

6. Choose **Save**.

To disable cross-zone load balancing, set the CrossZoneLoadBalancing attribute of your load balancer to false.

To disable cross-zone load balancing using the AWS CLI

1. Use the following modify-load-balancer-attributes command:

```
1 aws elb modify-load-balancer-attributes --load-balancer-name my-loadbalancer --load-
    balancer-attributes "{\"CrossZoneLoadBalancing\":{\"Enabled\":false}}"
```

The following is an example response:

```
1  {
2      "LoadBalancerAttributes": {
3        "CrossZoneLoadBalancing": {
4            "Enabled": false
```

```
5          }
6      },
7      "LoadBalancerName": "my-loadbalancer"
8  }
```

2. (Optional) Use the following describe-load-balancer-attributes command to verify that cross-zone load balancing is disabled for your load balancer:

```
1  aws elb describe-load-balancer-attributes --load-balancer-name my-loadbalancer
```

The following is an example response:

```
1  {
2      "LoadBalancerAttributes": {
3          "ConnectionDraining": {
4              "Enabled": false,
5              "Timeout": 300
6          },
7          "CrossZoneLoadBalancing": {
8              "Enabled": false
9          },
10         "ConnectionSettings": {
11             "IdleTimeout": 60
12         },
13         "AccessLog": {
14             "Enabled": false
15         }
16     }
17 }
```

Configure Connection Draining for Your Classic Load Balancer

To ensure that a Classic Load Balancer stops sending requests to instances that are de-registering or unhealthy, while keeping the existing connections open, use *connection draining*. This enables the load balancer to complete in-flight requests made to instances that are de-registering or unhealthy.

When you enable connection draining, you can specify a maximum time for the load balancer to keep connections alive before reporting the instance as de-registered. The maximum timeout value can be set between 1 and 3,600 seconds (the default is 300 seconds). When the maximum time limit is reached, the load balancer forcibly closes connections to the de-registering instance.

While in-flight requests are being served, the load balancer reports the state of a de-registering instance as `InService: Instance deregistration currently in progress`. When the de-registering instance is finished serving all in-flight requests, or when the maximum timeout limit is reached, the load balancer reports the instance state as `OutOfService: Instance is not currently registered with the LoadBalancer`.

If an instance becomes unhealthy, the load balancer reports the instance state as `OutOfService`. If there are in-flight requests made to the unhealthy instance, they are completed. The maximum timeout limit does not apply to connections to unhealthy instances.

If your instances are part of an Auto Scaling group and connection draining is enabled for your load balancer, Auto Scaling waits for the in-flight requests to complete, or for the maximum timeout to expire, before terminating instances due to a scaling event or health check replacement.

You can disable connection draining if you want your load balancer to immediately close connections to the instances that are de-registering or have become unhealthy. When connection draining is disabled, any in-flight requests made to instances that are de-registering or unhealthy are not completed.

Topics

- Enable Connection Draining
- Disable Connection Draining

Enable Connection Draining

You can enable connection draining for your load balancer at any time.

To enable connection draining using the console

1. Open the Amazon EC2 console at https://console.aws.amazon.com/ec2/.

2. On the navigation pane, under **LOAD BALANCING**, choose **Load Balancers**.

3. Select your load balancer.

4. On the **Instances** tab, for **Connection Draining**, choose **(Edit)**.

5. On the **Configure Connection Draining** page, select **Enable Connection Draining**.

6. (Optional) For **Timeout**, type a value between 1 and 3,600 seconds.

7. Choose **Save**.

To enable connection draining using the AWS CLI
Use the following modify-load-balancer-attributes command:

```
1 aws elb modify-load-balancer-attributes --load-balancer-name my-loadbalancer --load-balancer-
    attributes "{\"ConnectionDraining\":{\"Enabled\":true,\"Timeout\":300}}"
```

The following is an example response:

```
1 {
2     "LoadBalancerAttributes": {
3         "ConnectionDraining": {
4             "Enabled": true,
5             "Timeout": 300
6         }
7     },
8     "LoadBalancerName": "my-loadbalancer"
9 }
```

Disable Connection Draining

You can disable connection draining for your load balancer at any time.

To disable connection draining using the console

1. Open the Amazon EC2 console at https://console.aws.amazon.com/ec2/.

2. On the navigation pane, under **LOAD BALANCING**, choose **Load Balancers**.

3. Select your load balancer.

4. On the **Instances** tab, for **Connection Draining**, choose (**Edit**).

5. On the **Configure Connection Draining** page, clear **Enable Connection Draining**.

6. Choose **Save**.

To disable connection draining using the AWS CLI
Use the following modify-load-balancer-attributes command:

```
1 aws elb modify-load-balancer-attributes --load-balancer-name my-loadbalancer --load-balancer-
    attributes "{\"ConnectionDraining\":{\"Enabled\":false}}"
```

The following is an example response:

```
1 {
2     "LoadBalancerAttributes": {
3         "ConnectionDraining": {
4             "Enabled": false,
5             "Timeout": 300
6         }
7     },
8     "LoadBalancerName": "my-loadbalancer"
9 }
```

Configure Proxy Protocol Support for Your Classic Load Balancer

Proxy Protocol is an Internet protocol used to carry connection information from the source requesting the connection to the destination for which the connection was requested. Elastic Load Balancing uses Proxy Protocol version 1, which uses a human-readable header format.

By default, when you use Transmission Control Protocol (TCP) for both front-end and back-end connections, your Classic Load Balancer forwards requests to the instances without modifying the request headers. If you enable Proxy Protocol, a human-readable header is added to the request header with connection information such as the source IP address, destination IP address, and port numbers. The header is then sent to the instance as part of the request.

Note
The AWS Management Console does not support enabling Proxy Protocol.

Topics

- Proxy Protocol Header
- Prerequisites for Enabling Proxy Protocol
- Enable Proxy Protocol Using the AWS CLI
- Disable Proxy Protocol Using the AWS CLI

Proxy Protocol Header

The Proxy Protocol header helps you identify the IP address of a client when you have a load balancer that uses TCP for back-end connections. Because load balancers intercept traffic between clients and your instances, the access logs from your instance contain the IP address of the load balancer instead of the originating client. You can parse the first line of the request to retrieve your client's IP address and the port number.

The address of the proxy in the header for IPv6 is the public IPv6 address of your load balancer. This IPv6 address matches the IP address that is resolved from your load balancer's DNS name, which begins with either `ipv6` or `dualstack`. If the client connects with IPv4, the address of the proxy in the header is the private IPv4 address of the load balancer, which is not resolvable through a DNS lookup outside of the EC2-Classic network.

The Proxy Protocol line is a single line that ends with a carriage return and line feed (`"\r\n"`), and has the following form:

```
1 PROXY_STRING + single space + INET_PROTOCOL + single space + CLIENT_IP + single space + PROXY_IP
    + single space + CLIENT_PORT + single space + PROXY_PORT + "\r\n"
```

Example: IPv4
The following is an example of the Proxy Protocol line for IPv4.

```
1 PROXY TCP4 198.51.100.22 203.0.113.7 35646 80\r\n
```

Example: IPv6 (EC2-Classic only)
The following is an example of the IPv6 Proxy Protocol line for IPv6.

```
1 PROXY TCP6 2001:DB8::21f:5bff:febf:ce22:8a2e 2001:DB8::12f:8baa:eafc:ce29:6b2e 35646 80\r\n
```

Prerequisites for Enabling Proxy Protocol

Before you begin, do the following:

- Confirm that your load balancer is not behind a proxy server with Proxy Protocol enabled. If Proxy Protocol is enabled on both the proxy server and the load balancer, the load balancer adds another header to the request, which already has a header from the proxy server. Depending on how your instance is configured, this duplication might result in errors.

- Confirm that your instances can process the Proxy Protocol information.
- Confirm that your listener settings support Proxy Protocol. For more information, see Listener Configurations for Classic Load Balancers.

Enable Proxy Protocol Using the AWS CLI

To enable Proxy Protocol, you need to create a policy of type `ProxyProtocolPolicyType` and then enable the policy on the instance port.

Use the following procedure to create a new policy for your load balancer of type `ProxyProtocolPolicyType`, set the newly created policy to the instance on port 80, and verify that the policy is enabled.

To enable proxy protocol for your load balancer

1. (Optional) Use the following describe-load-balancer-policy-types command to list the policies supported by Elastic Load Balancing:

```
1  aws elb describe-load-balancer-policy-types
```

The response includes the names and descriptions of the supported policy types. The following shows the output for the `ProxyProtocolPolicyType` type:

```
1  {
2      "PolicyTypeDescriptions": [
3          ...
4          {
5              "PolicyAttributeTypeDescriptions": [
6                  {
7                      "Cardinality": "ONE",
8                      "AttributeName": "ProxyProtocol",
9                      "AttributeType": "Boolean"
10                 }
11             ],
12             "PolicyTypeName": "ProxyProtocolPolicyType",
13             "Description": "Policy that controls whether to include the IP address and port
                   of the originating
14 request for TCP messages. This policy operates on TCP/SSL listeners only"
15         },
16         ...
17     ]
18 }
```

2. Use the following create-load-balancer-policy command to create a policy that enables Proxy Protocol:

```
1  aws elb create-load-balancer-policy --load-balancer-name my-loadbalancer --policy-name my-
       ProxyProtocol-policy --policy-type-name ProxyProtocolPolicyType --policy-attributes
       AttributeName=ProxyProtocol,AttributeValue=true
```

3. Use the following set-load-balancer-policies-for-backend-server command to enable the newly created policy on the specified port. Note that this command replaces the current set of enabled policies. Therefore, the `--policy-names` option must specify both the policy that you are adding to the list (for example, `my-ProxyProtocol-policy`) and any policies that are currently enabled (for example, `my-existing-policy`).

```
1  aws elb set-load-balancer-policies-for-backend-server --load-balancer-name my-loadbalancer
       --instance-port 80 --policy-names my-ProxyProtocol-policy my-existing-policy
```

4. (Optional) Use the following describe-load-balancers command to verify that Proxy Protocol is enabled:

```
1 aws elb describe-load-balancers --load-balancer-name my-loadbalancer
```

The response includes the following information, which shows that the my-ProxyProtocol-policy policy is associated with port 80.

```
1  {
2      "LoadBalancerDescriptions": [
3          {
4              ...
5              "BackendServerDescriptions": [
6                  {
7                      "InstancePort": 80,
8                      "PolicyNames": [
9                          "my-ProxyProtocol-policy"
10                     ]
11                 }
12             ],
13             ...
14         }
15     ]
16 }
```

Disable Proxy Protocol Using the AWS CLI

You can disable the policies associated with your instance and then enable them at a later time.

To disable the Proxy Protocol policy

1. Use the following set-load-balancer-policies-for-backend-server command to disable the Proxy Protocol policy by omitting it from the --policy-names option, but including the other policies that should remain enabled (for example, my-existing-policy).

```
1 aws elb set-load-balancer-policies-for-backend-server --load-balancer-name my-loadbalancer
    --instance-port 80 --policy-names my-existing-policy
```

If there are no other policies to enable, specify an empty string with --policy-names option as follows:

```
1 aws elb set-load-balancer-policies-for-backend-server --load-balancer-name my-loadbalancer
    --instance-port 80 --policy-names "[]"
```

2. (Optional) Use the following describe-load-balancers command to verify that the policy is disabled:

```
1 aws elb describe-load-balancers --load-balancer-name my-loadbalancer
```

The response includes the following information, which shows that no ports are associated with a policy.

```
1  {
2      "LoadBalancerDescriptions": [
3          {
4              ...
5              "BackendServerDescriptions": [],
6              ...
7          }
8      ]
9  }
```

Configure Sticky Sessions for Your Classic Load Balancer

By default, a Classic Load Balancer routes each request independently to the registered instance with the smallest load. However, you can use the *sticky session* feature (also known as *session affinity*), which enables the load balancer to bind a user's session to a specific instance. This ensures that all requests from the user during the session are sent to the same instance.

The key to managing sticky sessions is to determine how long your load balancer should consistently route the user's request to the same instance. If your application has its own session cookie, then you can configure Elastic Load Balancing so that the session cookie follows the duration specified by the application's session cookie. If your application does not have its own session cookie, then you can configure Elastic Load Balancing to create a session cookie by specifying your own stickiness duration.

Elastic Load Balancing creates a cookie, named AWSELB, that is used to map the session to the instance.

Requirements

- An HTTP/HTTPS load balancer.
- At least one healthy instance in each Availability Zone.

Compatibility

- The RFC for the path property of a cookie allows underscores. However, Elastic Load Balancing URI encodes underscore characters as %5F because some browsers, such as Internet Explorer 7, expect underscores to be URI encoded as %5F. Because of the potential to impact browsers that are currently working, Elastic Load Balancing continues to URI encode underscore characters. For example, if the cookie has the property `path=/my_path`, Elastic Load Balancing changes this property in the forwarded request to `path=/my%5Fpath`.
- You can't set the `secure` flag or `HttpOnly` flag on your duration-based session stickiness cookies. However, these cookies contain no sensitive data. Note that if you set the `secure` flag or `HttpOnly` flag on an application-controlled session stickiness cookie, it is also set on the AWSELB cookie.
- If you have a trailing semicolon in the `Set-Cookie` field of an application cookie, the load balancer ignores the cookie.

Topics

- Duration-Based Session Stickiness
- Application-Controlled Session Stickiness

Duration-Based Session Stickiness

The load balancer uses a special cookie to track the instance for each request to each listener. When the load balancer receives a request, it first checks to see if this cookie is present in the request. If so, the request is sent to the instance specified in the cookie. If there is no cookie, the load balancer chooses an instance based on the existing load balancing algorithm. A cookie is inserted into the response for binding subsequent requests from the same user to that instance. The stickiness policy configuration defines a cookie expiration, which establishes the duration of validity for each cookie. The load balancer does not refresh the expiry time of the cookie and does not check whether the cookie is expired before using it. After a cookie expires, the session is no longer sticky. The client should remove the cookie from its cookie store upon expiry.

If an instance fails or becomes unhealthy, the load balancer stops routing requests to that instance, and chooses a new healthy instance based on the existing load balancing algorithm. The request is routed to the new instance as if there is no cookie and the session is no longer sticky.

If a client switches to a listener with a different backend port, stickiness is lost.

To enable duration-based sticky sessions for a load balancer using the console

1. Open the Amazon EC2 console at https://console.aws.amazon.com/ec2/.

2. On the navigation pane, under **LOAD BALANCING**, choose **Load Balancers**.

3. Select your load balancer.

4. On the **Description** tab, choose **Edit stickiness**.

5. On the **Edit stickiness ** page, select **Enable load balancer generated cookie stickiness**.

6. (Optional) For **Expiration Period**, type the cookie expiration period, in seconds. If you do not specify an expiration period, the sticky session lasts for the duration of the browser session.

7. Choose **Save**.

To enable duration-based sticky sessions for a load balancer using the AWS CLI

1. Use the following create-lb-cookie-stickiness-policy command to create a load balancer-generated cookie stickiness policy with a cookie expiration period of 60 seconds:

```
1 aws elb create-lb-cookie-stickiness-policy --load-balancer-name my-loadbalancer --policy-
    name my-duration-cookie-policy --cookie-expiration-period 60
```

2. Use the following set-load-balancer-policies-of-listener command to enable session stickiness for the specified load balancer:

```
1 aws elb set-load-balancer-policies-of-listener --load-balancer-name my-loadbalancer --load-
    balancer-port 443 --policy-names my-duration-cookie-policy
```

Note

The `set-load-balancer-policies-of-listener` command replaces the current set of policies associated with the specified load balancer port. Every time you use this command, specify the `--policy-names` option to list all policies to enable.

1. (Optional) Use the following describe-load-balancers command to verify that the policy is enabled:

```
1 aws elb describe-load-balancers --load-balancer-name my-loadbalancer
```

The response includes the following information, which shows that the policy is enabled for the listener on the specified port:

```
1  {
2      "LoadBalancerDescriptions": [
3          {
4              ...
5              "ListenerDescriptions": [
6                  {
7                      "Listener": {
8                          "InstancePort": 443,
9                          "SSLCertificateId": "arn:aws:iam::123456789012:server-certificate/
                               my-server-certificate",
10                         "LoadBalancerPort": 443,
11                         "Protocol": "HTTPS",
12                         "InstanceProtocol": "HTTPS"
13                     },
14                     "PolicyNames": [
15                         "my-duration-cookie-policy",
16                         "ELBSecurityPolicy-2016-08"
17                     ]
18                 },
19                 ...
20             ],
21             ...
```

```
22          "Policies": {
23              "LBCookieStickinessPolicies": [
24                  {
25                      "PolicyName": "my-duration-cookie-policy",
26                      "CookieExpirationPeriod": 60
27                  }
28
29              ],
30              "AppCookieStickinessPolicies": [],
31              "OtherPolicies": [
32                  "ELBSecurityPolicy-2016-08"
33              ]
34          },
35          ...
36      }
37    ]
38 }
```

Application-Controlled Session Stickiness

The load balancer uses a special cookie to associate the session with the instance that handled the initial request, but follows the lifetime of the application cookie specified in the policy configuration. The load balancer only inserts a new stickiness cookie if the application response includes a new application cookie. The load balancer stickiness cookie does not update with each request. If the application cookie is explicitly removed or expires, the session stops being sticky until a new application cookie is issued.

If an instance fails or becomes unhealthy, the load balancer stops routing requests to that instance, and chooses a new healthy instance based on the existing load balancing algorithm. The load balancer treats the session as now "stuck" to the new healthy instance, and continues routing requests to that instance even if the failed instance comes back.

To enable application-controlled session stickiness using the console

1. Open the Amazon EC2 console at https://console.aws.amazon.com/ec2/.

2. On the navigation pane, under **LOAD BALANCING**, choose **Load Balancers**.

3. Select your load balancer.

4. On the **Description** tab, choose **Edit stickiness**.

5. On the **Edit stickiness** page, select **Enable application generated cookie stickiness**.

6. For **Cookie Name**, type the name of your application cookie.

7. Choose **Save**.

To enable application-controlled session stickiness using the AWS CLI

1. Use the following create-app-cookie-stickiness-policy command to create an application-generated cookie stickiness policy:

```
1 aws elb create-app-cookie-stickiness-policy --load-balancer-name my-loadbalancer --policy-
   name my-app-cookie-policy --cookie-name my-app-cookie
```

2. Use the following set-load-balancer-policies-of-listener command to enable session stickiness for a load balancer:

```
1 aws elb set-load-balancer-policies-of-listener --load-balancer-name my-loadbalancer --load-
   balancer-port 443 --policy-names my-app-cookie-policy
```

Note

The `set-load-balancer-policies-of-listener` command replaces the current set of policies associated with the specified load balancer port. Every time you use this command, specify the `--policy-names` option to list all policies to enable.

1. (Optional) Use the following describe-load-balancers command to verify that the sticky policy is enabled:

```
1 aws elb describe-load-balancers --load-balancer-name my-loadbalancer
```

2. The response includes the following information, which shows that the policy is enabled for the listener on the specified port:

```
1  {
2      "LoadBalancerDescriptions": [
3          {
4              ...
5              "ListenerDescriptions": [
6                  {
7                      "Listener": {
8                          "InstancePort": 443,
9                          "SSLCertificateId": "arn:aws:iam::123456789012:server-certificate/
                             my-server-certificate",
10                         "LoadBalancerPort": 443,
11                         "Protocol": "HTTPS",
12                         "InstanceProtocol": "HTTPS"
13                     },
14                     "PolicyNames": [
15                         "my-app-cookie-policy",
16                         "ELBSecurityPolicy-2016-08"
17                     ]
18                 },
19                 {
20                     "Listener": {
21                         "InstancePort": 80,
22                         "LoadBalancerPort": 80,
23                         "Protocol": "TCP",
24                         "InstanceProtocol": "TCP"
25                     },
26                     "PolicyNames": []
27                 }
28             ],
29             ...
30             "Policies": {
31                 "LBCookieStickinessPolicies": [],
32                 "AppCookieStickinessPolicies": [
33                     {
34                         "PolicyName": "my-app-cookie-policy",
35                         "CookieName": "my-app-cookie"
36                     }
37
38                 ],
39                 "OtherPolicies": [
40                     "ELBSecurityPolicy-2016-08"
41                 ]
42             },
43             ...
```

```
44        }
45     ]
46 }
```

Tag Your Classic Load Balancer

Tags help you to categorize your load balancers in different ways, for example, by purpose, owner, or environment.

You can add multiple tags to each Classic Load Balancer. Tag keys must be unique for each load balancer. If you add a tag with a key that is already associated with the load balancer, it updates the value of that tag.

When you are finished with a tag, you can remove it from your load balancer.

Topics

- Tag Restrictions
- Add a Tag
- Remove a Tag

Tag Restrictions

The following basic restrictions apply to tags:

- Maximum number of tags per resource—50
- Maximum key length—127 Unicode characters
- Maximum value length—255 Unicode characters
- Tag keys and values are case sensitive. Allowed characters are letters, spaces, and numbers representable in UTF-8, plus the following special characters: + - = . _ : / @. Do not use leading or trailing spaces.
- Do not use the `aws:` prefix in your tag names or values because it is reserved for AWS use. You can't edit or delete tag names or values with this prefix. Tags with this prefix do not count against your tags per resource limit.

Add a Tag

You can add tags to your load balancer at any time.

To add a tag using the console

1. Open the Amazon EC2 console at https://console.aws.amazon.com/ec2/.

2. On the navigation pane, under **LOAD BALANCING**, choose **Load Balancers**.

3. Select your load balancer.

4. On the **Tags** tab, choose **Add/Edit Tags**.

5. On the **Add/Edit Tags** page, for each tag, choose **Create Tag** and then specify a key and a value.

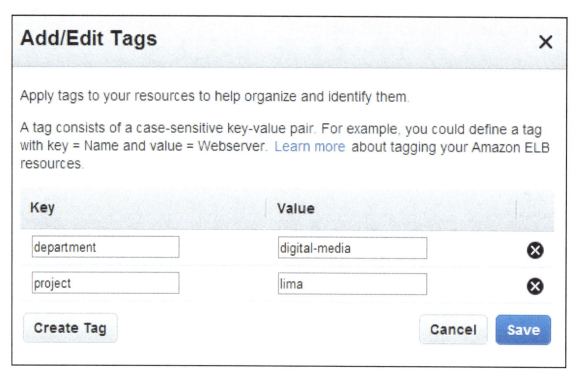

6. After you have finished adding tags, choose **Save**.

To add a tag using the AWS CLI

Use the following add-tags command to add the specified tag:

```
1 aws elb add-tags --load-balancer-name my-loadbalancer --tag "Key=project,Value=lima"
```

Remove a Tag

You can remove tags from your load balancer whenever you are finished with them.

To remove a tag using the console

1. Open the Amazon EC2 console at https://console.aws.amazon.com/ec2/.

2. On the navigation pane, under **LOAD BALANCING**, choose **Load Balancers**.

3. Select your load balancer.

4. On the **Tags** tab, choose **Add/Edit Tags**.

5. On the **Add/Edit Tags** page, choose the remove icon of the tag.

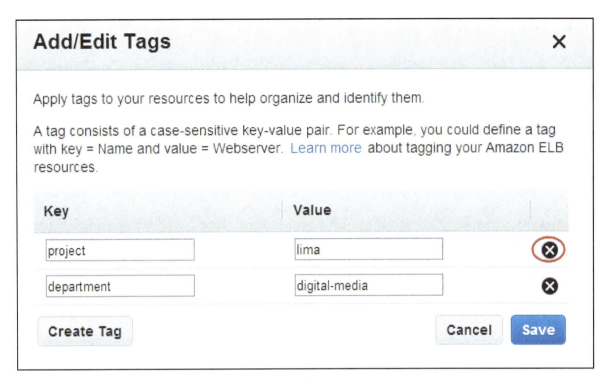

6. After you are have finished removing tags, choose **Save**.

To remove a tag using the AWS CLI
Use the following remove-tags command to remove the tag with the specified key:

```
1 aws elb remove-tags --load-balancer-name my-loadbalancer --tag project
```

Configure a Custom Domain Name for Your Classic Load Balancer

Each Classic Load Balancer receives a default Domain Name System (DNS) name. This DNS name includes the name of the AWS region in which the load balancer is created. For example, if you create a load balancer named `my-loadbalancer` in the US West (Oregon) region, your load balancer receives a DNS name such as `my-loadbalancer-1234567890.us-west-2.elb.amazonaws.com`. To access the website on your instances, you paste this DNS name into the address field of a web browser. However, this DNS name is not easy for your customers to remember and use.

If you'd prefer to use a friendly DNS name for your load balancer, such as `www.example.com`, instead of the default DNS name, you can create a custom domain name and associate it with the DNS name for your load balancer. When a client makes a request using this custom domain name, the DNS server resolves it to the DNS name for your load balancer.

Topics

- Associating Your Custom Domain Name with Your Load Balancer Name
- Configure DNS Failover for Your Load Balancer
- Disassociating Your Custom Domain Name from Your Load Balancer

Associating Your Custom Domain Name with Your Load Balancer Name

First, if you haven't already done so, register your domain name. The Internet Corporation for Assigned Names and Numbers (ICANN) manages domain names on the Internet. You register a domain name using a *domain name registrar*, an ICANN-accredited organization that manages the registry of domain names. The website for your registrar will provide detailed instructions and pricing information for registering your domain name. For more information, see the following resources:

- To use Amazon Route 53 to register a domain name, see Registering Domain Names Using Route 53 in the *Amazon Route 53 Developer Guide*.
- For a list of accredited registrars, see the Accredited Registrar Directory.

Next, use your DNS service, such as your domain registrar, to create a CNAME record to route queries to your load balancer. For more information, see the documentation for your DNS service.

Alternatively, you can use Route 53 as your DNS service. You create a *hosted zone*, which contains information about how to route traffic on the Internet for your domain, and an *alias resource record set*, which routes queries for your domain name to your load balancer. Route 53 doesn't charge for DNS queries for alias record sets, and you can use alias record sets to route DNS queries to your load balancer for the zone apex of your domain (for example, `example.com`). For information about transferring DNS services for existing domains to Route 53, see Configuring Route 53 as Your DNS Service in the *Amazon Route 53 Developer Guide*.

To create a hosted zone and an alias record set for your domain using Route 53

1. Open the Route 53 console at https://console.aws.amazon.com/route53/.

2. If you are new to Route 53, you see a welcome page; choose **Get Started Now** under **DNS Management**. Otherwise, choose **Hosted Zones** in the navigation pane.

3. Choose **Create Hosted Zone**.

4. For **Create Hosted Zone**, do the following:

    1. For **Domain Name**, type your domain name.

    2. Leave the default type, Public Hosted Zone, and optionally enter a comment.

    3. Choose **Create**.

5. Select the hosted zone that you just created for your domain.

6. Choose **Go to Record Sets**.

7. Choose **Create Record Set**.

8. For **Create Record Set**, do the following:

    1. Leave the default name, which is the name of your domain.

    2. For **Type**, select **A — IPv4 address**.

    3. For **Alias**, choose **Yes**. An alias enables Route 53 to associate your domain name with an AWS resource, such as a load balancer.

    4. Choose **Alias Target**. Select your load balancer from the list. The console adds the `dualstack` prefix.

    5. For **Routing Policy**, select **Simple**.

    6. Leave **Evaluate Target Health** set to **No**.

    7. Choose **Create**.

Configure DNS Failover for Your Load Balancer

If you use Route 53 to route DNS queries to your load balancer, you can also configure DNS failover for your load balancer using Route 53. In a failover configuration, Route 53 checks the health of the registered EC2 instances for the load balancer to determine whether they are available. If there are no healthy EC2 instances registered with the load balancer, or if the load balancer itself is unhealthy, Route 53 routes traffic to another available resource, such as a healthy load balancer or a static website in Amazon S3.

For example, suppose that you have a web application for `www.example.com`, and you want redundant instances running behind two load balancers residing in different regions. You want the traffic to be primarily routed to the load balancer in one region, and you want to use the load balancer in the other region as a backup during failures. If you configure DNS failover, you can specify your primary and secondary (backup) load balancers. Route 53 directs traffic to the primary load balancer if it is available, or to the secondary load balancer otherwise.

To configure DNS failover for two load balancers using Route 53

1. Open the Route 53 console at https://console.aws.amazon.com/route53/.

2. In the navigation pane, choose **Hosted Zones**.

3. Select your hosted zone.

4. Choose **Go to Record Sets**.

5. Choose **Create Record Set**.

6. For **Name**, the default value is the name of your domain (for example, `example.com`). To route DNS queries for a subdomain (for example, `www.example.com`) to your load balancer, type the name of the subdomain.

7. For **Type**, select **A - IPv4 address**.

8. For **Alias**, select **Yes**

9. For **Alias Target**, select your primary load balancer. The console adds the `dualstack` prefix.

    Note that the value of **Alias Hosted Zone ID** is based on the load balancer that you selected.

10. For **Routing Policy**, select **Failover**.

11. For **Failover Record Type**, select **Primary**.

12. For **Set ID**, type an ID for the record set or use the default value.

13. For **Evaluate Target Health**, select **Yes**.

14. For **Associate with Health Check**, select **No**.

15. Choose **Create**.

16. Repeat the same steps to create an alias record set for your secondary load balancer, with the following exceptions:
    - For **Alias Target**, select your secondary load balancer.
    - For **Failover Record Type**, select **Secondary**.
    - For **Evaluate Target Health**, select **Yes** to evaluate the health of the secondary load balancer. If the secondary load balancer is unhealthy, Route 53 routes traffic to the primary load balancer. If you select **No**, Route 53 assumes that the secondary load balancer is healthy and routes traffic to it whenever the primary load balancer is unhealthy.

For more information, see Configuring Route 53 Active-Active and Active-Passive Failover in the *Amazon Route 53 Developer Guide*.

Disassociating Your Custom Domain Name from Your Load Balancer

You can disassociate your custom domain name from a load balancer instance by first deleting the resource record sets in your hosted zone and then deleting the hosted zone. For more information, see Creating, Changing, and Deleting Resource Record Sets and Deleting a Hosted Zone in the *Amazon Route 53 Developer Guide*.

Monitor Your Classic Load Balancer

You can use the following features to monitor your load balancers, analyze traffic patterns, and troubleshoot issues with your load balancers and back-end instances.

CloudWatch metrics

Elastic Load Balancing publishes data points to Amazon CloudWatch about your load balancers and back-end instances. CloudWatch enables you to retrieve statistics about those data points as an ordered set of time-series data, known as *metrics*. You can use these metrics to verify that your system is performing as expected. For more information, see CloudWatch Metrics for Your Classic Load Balancer.

Elastic Load Balancing access logs

The access logs for Elastic Load Balancing capture detailed information for requests made to your load balancer and stores them as log files in the Amazon S3 bucket that you specify. Each log contains details such as the time a request was received, the client's IP address, latencies, request path, and server responses. You can use these access logs to analyze traffic patterns and to troubleshoot your back-end applications. For more information, see Access Logs for Your Classic Load Balancer.

CloudTrail logs

AWS CloudTrail enables you to keep track of the calls made to the Elastic Load Balancing API by or on behalf of your AWS account. CloudTrail stores the information in log files in the Amazon S3 bucket that you specify. You can use these log files to monitor activity of your load balancers by determining which requests were made, the source IP addresses where the requests came from, who made the request, when the request was made, and so on. For more information, see AWS CloudTrail Logging for Your Classic Load Balancer.

CloudWatch Metrics for Your Classic Load Balancer

Elastic Load Balancing publishes data points to Amazon CloudWatch for your load balancers and your back-end instances. CloudWatch enables you to retrieve statistics about those data points as an ordered set of time-series data, known as *metrics*. Think of a metric as a variable to monitor, and the data points as the values of that variable over time. For example, you can monitor the total number of healthy EC2 instances for a load balancer over a specified time period. Each data point has an associated time stamp and an optional unit of measurement.

You can use metrics to verify that your system is performing as expected. For example, you can create a CloudWatch alarm to monitor a specified metric and initiate an action (such as sending a notification to an email address) if the metric goes outside what you consider an acceptable range.

Elastic Load Balancing reports metrics to CloudWatch only when requests are flowing through the load balancer. If there are requests flowing through the load balancer, Elastic Load Balancing measures and sends its metrics in 60-second intervals. If there are no requests flowing through the load balancer or no data for a metric, the metric is not reported.

For more information about Amazon CloudWatch, see the *Amazon CloudWatch User Guide*.

Topics

- Classic Load Balancer Metrics
- Metric Dimensions for Classic Load Balancers
- Statistics for Classic Load Balancer Metrics
- View CloudWatch Metrics for Your Load Balancer
- Create CloudWatch Alarms for Your Load Balancer

Classic Load Balancer Metrics

The `AWS/ELB` namespace includes the following metrics.

Metric	Description
BackendConnectionErrors	The number of connections that were not successfully established between the load balancer and the registered instances. Because the load balancer retries the connection when there are errors, this count can exceed the request rate. Note that this count also includes any connection errors related to health checks. **Reporting criteria**: There is a nonzero value **Statistics**: The most useful statistic is Sum. Note that Average, Minimum, and Maximum are reported per load balancer node and are not typically useful. However, the difference between the minimum and maximum (or peak to average or average to trough) might be useful to determine whether a load balancer node is an outlier. **Example**: Suppose that your load balancer has 2 instances in us-west-2a and 2 instances in us-west-2b, and that attempts to connect to 1 instance in us-west-2a result in back-end connection errors. The sum for us-west-2a includes these connection errors, while the sum for us-west-2b does not include them. Therefore, the sum for the load balancer equals the sum for us-west-2a.
HealthyHostCount	The number of healthy instances registered with your load balancer. A newly registered instance is considered healthy after it passes the first health check. If cross-zone load balancing is enabled, the number of healthy instances for the LoadBalancerName dimension is calculated across all Availability Zones. Otherwise, it is calculated per Availability Zone. **Reporting criteria**: There are registered instances **Statistics**: The most useful statistics are Average and Maximum. These statistics are determined by the load balancer nodes. Note that some load balancer nodes might determine that an instance is unhealthy for a brief period while other nodes determine that it is healthy. **Example**: Suppose that your load balancer has 2 instances in us-west-2a and 2 instances in us-west-2b, us-west-2a has 1 unhealthy instance, and us-west-2b has no unhealthy instances. With the AvailabilityZone dimension, there is an average of 1 healthy and 1 unhealthy instance in us-west-2a, and an average of 2 healthy and 0 unhealthy instances in us-west-2b.

Metric	Description
HTTPCode_Backend_2XX, HTTPCode_Backend_3XX, HTTPCode_Backend_4XX, HTTPCode_Backend_5XX	[HTTP listener] The number of HTTP response codes generated by registered instances. This count does not include any response codes generated by the load balancer. **Reporting criteria**: There is a nonzero value **Statistics**: The most useful statistic is Sum. Note that Minimum, Maximum, and Average are all 1. **Example**: Suppose that your load balancer has 2 instances in us-west-2a and 2 instances in us-west-2b, and that requests sent to 1 instance in us-west-2a result in HTTP 500 responses. The sum for us-west-2a includes these error responses, while the sum for us-west-2b does not include them. Therefore, the sum for the load balancer equals the sum for us-west-2a.
HTTPCode_ELB_4XX	[HTTP listener] The number of HTTP 4XX client error codes generated by the load balancer. Client errors are generated when a request is malformed or incomplete. **Reporting criteria**: There is a nonzero value **Statistics**: The most useful statistic is Sum. Note that Minimum, Maximum, and Average are all 1. **Example**: Suppose that your load balancer has us-west-2a and us-west-2b enabled, and that client requests include a malformed request URL. As a result, client errors would likely increase in all Availability Zones. The sum for the load balancer is the sum of the values for the Availability Zones.
HTTPCode_ELB_5XX	[HTTP listener] The number of HTTP 5XX server error codes generated by the load balancer. This count does not include any response codes generated by the registered instances. The metric is reported if there are no healthy instances registered to the load balancer, or if the request rate exceeds the capacity of the instances (spillover) or the load balancer. **Reporting criteria**: There is a nonzero value **Statistics**: The most useful statistic is Sum. Note that Minimum, Maximum, and Average are all 1. **Example**: Suppose that your load balancer has us-west-2a and us-west-2b enabled, and that instances in us-west-2a are experiencing high latency and are slow to respond to requests. As a result, the surge queue for the load balancer nodes in us-west-2a fills and clients receive a 503 error. If us-west-2b continues to respond normally, the sum for the load balancer equals the sum for us-west-2a.

Metric	Description
Latency	[HTTP listener] The total time elapsed, in seconds, from the time the load balancer sent the request to a registered instance until the instance started to send the response headers. [TCP listener] The total time elapsed, in seconds, for the load balancer to successfully establish a connection to a registered instance. **Reporting criteria**: There is a nonzero value **Statistics**: The most useful statistic is Average. Use Maximum to determine whether some requests are taking substantially longer than the average. Note that Minimum is typically not useful. **Example**: Suppose that your load balancer has 2 instances in us-west-2a and 2 instances in us-west-2b, and that requests sent to 1 instance in us-west-2a have a higher latency. The average for us-west-2a has a higher value than the average for us-west-2b.
RequestCount	The number of requests completed or connections made during the specified interval (1 or 5 minutes). [HTTP listener] The number of requests received and routed, including HTTP error responses from the registered instances. [TCP listener] The number of connections made to the registered instances. **Reporting criteria**: There is a nonzero value **Statistics**: The most useful statistic is Sum. Note that Minimum, Maximum, and Average all return 1. **Example**: Suppose that your load balancer has 2 instances in us-west-2a and 2 instances in us-west-2b, and that 100 requests are sent to the load balancer. There are 60 requests sent to us-west-2a, with each instance receiving 30 requests, and 40 requests sent to us-west-2b, with each instance receiving 20 requests. With the AvailabilityZone dimension, there is a sum of 60 requests in us-west-2a and 40 requests in us-west-2b. With the LoadBalancerName dimension, there is a sum of 100 requests.

Metric	Description
SpilloverCount	The total number of requests that were rejected because the surge queue is full. [HTTP listener] The load balancer returns an HTTP 503 error code. [TCP listener] The load balancer closes the connection. **Reporting criteria**: There is a nonzero value **Statistics**: The most useful statistic is `Sum`. Note that `Average`, `Minimum`, and `Maximum` are reported per load balancer node and are not typically useful. **Example**: Suppose that your load balancer has us-west-2a and us-west-2b enabled, and that instances in us-west-2a are experiencing high latency and are slow to respond to requests. As a result, the surge queue for the load balancer node in us-west-2a fills, resulting in spillover. If us-west-2b continues to respond normally, the sum for the load balancer will be the same as the sum for us-west-2a.
SurgeQueueLength	The total number of requests that are pending routing. The load balancer queues a request if it is unable to establish a connection with a healthy instance in order to route the request. The maximum size of the queue is 1,024. Additional requests are rejected when the queue is full. For more information, see `SpilloverCount`. **Reporting criteria**: There is a nonzero value. **Statistics**: The most useful statistic is `Maximum`, because it represents the peak of queued requests. The `Average` statistic can be useful in combination with `Minimum` and `Maximum` to determine the range of queued requests. Note that `Sum` is not useful. **Example**: Suppose that your load balancer has us-west-2a and us-west-2b enabled, and that instances in us-west-2a are experiencing high latency and are slow to respond to requests. As a result, the surge queue for the load balancer nodes in us-west-2a fills, with clients likely experiencing increased response times. If this continues, the load balancer will likely have spillovers (see the `SpilloverCount` metric). If us-west-2b continues to respond normally, the `max` for the load balancer will be the same as the `max` for us-west-2a.

Metric	Description
UnHealthyHostCount	The number of unhealthy instances registered with your load balancer. An instance is considered unhealthy after it exceeds the unhealthy threshold configured for health checks. An unhealthy instance is considered healthy again after it meets the healthy threshold configured for health checks. **Reporting criteria**: There are registered instances **Statistics**: The most useful statistics are `Average` and `Minimum`. These statistics are determined by the load balancer nodes. Note that some load balancer nodes might determine that an instance is unhealthy for a brief period while other nodes determine that it is healthy. **Example**: See `HealthyHostCount`.

The following metrics enable you to estimate your costs if you migrate a Classic Load Balancer to an Application Load Balancer. These metrics are intended for informational use only, not for use with CloudWatch alarms. Note that if your Classic Load Balancer has multiple listeners, these metrics are aggregated across the listeners.

These estimates are based on a load balancer with one default rule and a certificate that is 2K in size. If you use a certificate that is 4K or greater in size, we recommend that you estimate your costs as follows: create an Application Load Balancer based on your Classic Load Balancer using the migration tool and monitor the `ConsumedLCUs` metric for the Application Load Balancer. For more information, see Migrate from a Classic Load Balancer to an Application Load Balancer in the *Elastic Load Balancing User Guide*.

Metric	Description
EstimatedALBActiveConnectionCount	The estimated number of concurrent TCP connections active from clients to the load balancer and from the load balancer to targets.
EstimatedALBConsumedLCUs	The estimated number of load balancer capacity units (LCU) used by an Application Load Balancer. You pay for the number of LCUs that you use per hour. For more information, see Elastic Load Balancing Pricing.
EstimatedALBNewConnectionCount	The estimated number of new TCP connections established from clients to the load balancer and from the load balancer to targets.
EstimatedProcessedBytes	The estimated number of bytes processed by an Application Load Balancer.

Metric Dimensions for Classic Load Balancers

To filter the metrics for your Classic Load Balancer, use the following dimensions.

Dimension	Description
AvailabilityZone	Filter the metric data by the specified Availability Zone.

Dimension	Description
LoadBalancerName	Filter the metric data by the specified load balancer.

Statistics for Classic Load Balancer Metrics

CloudWatch provides statistics based on the metric data points published by Elastic Load Balancing. Statistics are metric data aggregations over specified period of time. When you request statistics, the returned data stream is identified by the metric name and dimension. A dimension is a name/value pair that uniquely identifies a metric. For example, you can request statistics for all the healthy EC2 instances behind a load balancer launched in a specific Availability Zone.

The `Minimum` and `Maximum` statistics reflect the minimum and maximum reported by the individual load balancer nodes. For example, suppose there are 2 load balancer nodes. One node has `HealthyHostCount` with a `Minimum` of 2, a `Maximum` of 10, and an `Average` of 6, while the other node has `HealthyHostCount` with a `Minimum` of 1, a `Maximum` of 5, and an `Average` of 3. Therefore, the load balancer has a `Minimum` of 1, a `Maximum` of 10, and an `Average` of about 4.

The `Sum` statistic is the aggregate value across all load balancer nodes. Because metrics include multiple reports per period, `Sum` is only applicable to metrics that are aggregated across all load balancer nodes, such as `RequestCount`, `HTTPCode_ELB_XXX`, `HTTPCode_Backend_XXX`, `BackendConnectionErrors`, and `SpilloverCount`.

The `SampleCount` statistic is the number of samples measured. Because metrics are gathered based on sampling intervals and events, this statistic is typically not useful. For example, with `HealthyHostCount`, `SampleCount` is based on the number of samples that each load balancer node reports, not the number of healthy hosts.

A percentile indicates the relative standing of a value in a data set. You can specify any percentile, using up to two decimal places (for example, p95.45). For example, the 95th percentile means that 95 percent of the data is below this value and 5 percent is above. Percentiles are often used to isolate anomalies. For example, suppose that an application serves the majority of requests from a cache in 1-2 ms, but in 100-200 ms if the cache is empty. The maximum reflects the slowest case, around 200 ms. The average doesn't indicate the distribution of the data. Percentiles provide a more meaningful view of the application's performance. By using the 99th percentile as an Auto Scaling trigger or a CloudWatch alarm, you can target that no more than 1 percent of requests take longer than 2 ms to process.

View CloudWatch Metrics for Your Load Balancer

You can view the CloudWatch metrics for your load balancers using the Amazon EC2 console. These metrics are displayed as monitoring graphs. The monitoring graphs show data points if the load balancer is active and receiving requests.

Alternatively, you can view metrics for your load balancer using the CloudWatch console.

To view metrics using the Amazon EC2 console

1. Open the Amazon EC2 console at https://console.aws.amazon.com/ec2/.

2. On the navigation pane, under **LOAD BALANCING**, choose **Load Balancers**.

3. Select your load balancer.

4. Choose the **Monitoring** tab.

5. (Optional) To filter the results by time, select a time range from **Showing data for**.

6. To get a larger view of a single metric, select its graph. The following metrics are available:

   - Healthy Hosts — `HealthyHostCount`

- Unhealthy Hosts — `UnHealthyHostCount`
- Average Latency — `Latency`
- Sum Requests — `RequestCount`
- Backend Connection Errors — `BackendConnectionErrors`
- Surge Queue Length — `SurgeQueueLength`
- Spillover Count — `SpilloverCount`
- Sum HTTP 2XXs — `HTTPCode_Backend_2XX`
- Sum HTTP 4XXs — `HTTPCode_Backend_4XX`
- Sum HTTP 5XXs — `HTTPCode_Backend_5XX`
- Sum ELB HTTP 4XXs — `HTTPCode_ELB_4XX`
- Sum ELB HTTP 5XXs — `HTTPCode_ELB_5XX`

To view metrics using the CloudWatch console

1. Open the CloudWatch console at https://console.aws.amazon.com/cloudwatch/.

2. In the navigation pane, choose **Metrics**.

3. Select the **ELB** namespace.

4. Do one of the following:

   - Select a metric dimension to view metrics by load balancer, by Availability Zone, or across all load balancers.
   - To view a metric across all dimensions, type its name in the search field.
   - To view the metrics for a single load balancer, type its name in the search field.
   - To view the metrics for a single Availability Zone, type its name in the search field.

Create CloudWatch Alarms for Your Load Balancer

An alarm watches a single metric over the time period that you specify. Depending on the value of the metric relative to a threshold that you define, the alarm can send one or more notifications using Amazon SNS, a service that enables applications, end users, and devices to instantly send and receive notifications. For more information, see Get Started with Amazon SNS.

An alarm sends notifications to Amazon SNS when the specified metric reaches the defined range and remains in that range for a specified period of time. An alarm has three possible states:

- `OK`—The value of the metric is within the range you've specified.
- `ALARM`—The value of the metric is outside the range that you've specified for the specified period of time.
- `INSUFFICIENT_DATA`—Either the metric is not yet available or there is not enough data to determine the alarm state.

Whenever the state of an alarm changes, CloudWatch uses Amazon SNS to send a notification to the email addresses that you specified.

Use the following procedure to create an alarm for your load balancer using the Amazon EC2 console. The alarm sends notifications to an SNS topic whenever the load balancer's latency is above 120 seconds for 1 consecutive period of 5 minutes. Note that a short period creates a more sensitive alarm, while a longer period can mitigate brief spikes in a metric.

Note
Alternately, you can create an alarm for your load balancer using the CloudWatch console. For more information, see Send Email Based on Load Balancer Alarm in the *Amazon CloudWatch User Guide*.

To create an alarm for your load balancer

1. Open the Amazon EC2 console at https://console.aws.amazon.com/ec2/.

2. On the navigation pane, under **LOAD BALANCING**, choose **Load Balancers**.

3. Select your load balancer.

4. On the **Monitoring** tab, choose **Create Alarm**.

5. If you have an SNS topic that you want to use, select it from **Send a notification to**. Otherwise, create an SNS topic as follows:

   1. Choose **create topic**.

   2. For **Send a notification to**, type a name for your topic.

   3. For **With these recipients**, type the email addresses of the recipients to notify, separated by commas. You can enter up to 10 email addresses. Each recipient receives an email from Amazon SNS with a link to subscribe to the SNS topic in order to receive notifications.

6. Define the threshold for your alarm as follows. For **Whenever**, select **Average** and **Average Latency**. For **Is**, select > and enter 120. For **For at least**, type 1 and select a consecutive period of **5 minutes**.

7. For **Name of alarm**, a name is automatically generated for you. If you prefer, you can type a different name.

8. Choose **Create Alarm**.

Access Logs for Your Classic Load Balancer

Elastic Load Balancing provides access logs that capture detailed information about requests sent to your load balancer. Each log contains information such as the time the request was received, the client's IP address, latencies, request paths, and server responses. You can use these access logs to analyze traffic patterns and to troubleshoot issues.

Access logging is an optional feature of Elastic Load Balancing that is disabled by default. After you enable access logging for your load balancer, Elastic Load Balancing captures the logs and stores them in the Amazon S3 bucket that you specify. You can disable access logging at any time.

There is no additional charge for access logs. You will be charged storage costs for Amazon S3, but will not be charged for the bandwidth used by Elastic Load Balancing to send log files to Amazon S3. For more information about storage costs, see Amazon S3 Pricing.

Topics

- Access Log Files
- Access Log Entries
- Processing Access Logs
- Enable Access Logs for Your Classic Load Balancer
- Disable Access Logs for Your Classic Load Balancer

Access Log Files

Elastic Load Balancing publishes a log file for each load balancer node at the interval you specify. You can specify a publishing interval of either 5 minutes or 60 minutes when you enable the access log for your load balancer. By default, Elastic Load Balancing publishes logs at a 60-minute interval. If the interval is set for 5 minutes, the logs are published at 1:05, 1:10, 1:15, and so on. The start of log delivery is delayed up to 5 minutes if the interval is set to 5 minutes, and up to 15 minutes if the interval is set to 60 minutes. You can modify the publishing interval at any time.

The load balancer can deliver multiple logs for the same period. This usually happens if the site has high traffic, multiple load balancer nodes, and a short log publishing interval.

The file names of the access logs use the following format:

```
1 bucket[/prefix]/AWSLogs/aws-account-id/elasticloadbalancing/region/yyyy/mm/dd/aws-account-
      id_elasticloadbalancing_region_load-balancer-name_end-time_ip-address_random-string.log
```

bucket
The name of the S3 bucket.

prefix
The prefix (logical hierarchy) in the bucket. If you don't specify a prefix, the logs are placed at the root level of the bucket.

aws-account-id
The AWS account ID of the owner.

region
The region for your load balancer and S3 bucket.

yyyy/mm/dd
The date that the log was delivered.

load-balancer-name
The name of the load balancer.

end-time
The date and time that the logging interval ended. For example, an end time of 20140215T2340Z contains entries for requests made between 23:35 and 23:40 if the publishing interval is 5 minutes.

ip-address
The IP address of the load balancer node that handled the request. For an internal load balancer, this is a private IP address.

random-string
A system-generated random string.

The following is an example log file name:

```
1 s3://my-loadbalancer-logs/my-app/AWSLogs/123456789012/elasticloadbalancing/us-west
     -2/2014/02/15/123456789012_elasticloadbalancing_us-west-2_my-loadbalancer_20140215T2340Z_172
     .160.001.192_20sg8hgm.log
```

You can store your log files in your bucket for as long as you want, but you can also define Amazon S3 lifecycle rules to archive or delete log files automatically. For more information, see Object Lifecycle Management in the *Amazon Simple Storage Service Developer Guide.*

Access Log Entries

Elastic Load Balancing logs requests sent to the load balancer, including requests that never made it to the back-end instances. For example, if a client sends a malformed request, or there are no healthy instances to respond, the requests are still logged.

Important
Elastic Load Balancing logs requests on a best-effort basis. We recommend that you use access logs to understand the nature of the requests, not as a complete accounting of all requests.

Syntax

Each log entry contains the details of a single request made to the load balancer. All fields in the log entry are delimited by spaces. Each entry in the log file has the following format:

```
1 timestamp elb client:port backend:port request_processing_time backend_processing_time
     response_processing_time elb_status_code backend_status_code received_bytes sent_bytes "
     request" "user_agent" ssl_cipher ssl_protocol
```

The following table describes the fields of an access log entry.

Field	Description
timestamp	The time when the load balancer received the request from the client, in ISO 8601 format.
elb	The name of the load balancer
client:port	The IP address and port of the requesting client.
backend:port	The IP address and port of the registered instance that processed this request. If the load balancer can't send the request to a registered instance, or if the instance closes the connection before a response can be sent, this value is set to -. This value can also be set to - if the registered instance does not respond before the idle timeout.

110

Field	Description
request_processing_time	[HTTP listener] The total time elapsed, in seconds, from the time the load balancer received the request until the time it sent it to a registered instance. [TCP listener] The total time elapsed, in seconds, from the time the load balancer accepted a TCP/SSL connection from a client to the time the load balancer sends the first byte of data to a registered instance. This value is set to -1 if the load balancer can't dispatch the request to a registered instance. This can happen if the registered instance closes the connection before the idle timeout or if the client sends a malformed request. Additionally, for TCP listeners, this can happen if the client establishes a connection with the load balancer but does not send any data. This value can also be set to -1 if the registered instance does not respond before the idle timeout.
backend_processing_time	[HTTP listener] The total time elapsed, in seconds, from the time the load balancer sent the request to a registered instance until the instance started to send the response headers. [TCP listener] The total time elapsed, in seconds, for the load balancer to successfully establish a connection to a registered instance. This value is set to -1 if the load balancer can't dispatch the request to a registered instance. This can happen if the registered instance closes the connection before the idle timeout or if the client sends a malformed request. This value can also be set to -1 if the registered instance does not respond before the idle timeout.
response_processing_time	[HTTP listener] The total time elapsed (in seconds) from the time the load balancer received the response header from the registered instance until it started to send the response to the client. This includes both the queuing time at the load balancer and the connection acquisition time from the load balancer to the client. [TCP listener] The total time elapsed, in seconds, from the time the load balancer received the first byte from the registered instance until it started to send the response to the client. This value is set to -1 if the load balancer can't dispatch the request to a registered instance. This can happen if the registered instance closes the connection before the idle timeout or if the client sends a malformed request. This value can also be set to -1 if the registered instance does not respond before the idle timeout.

Field	Description
elb_status_code	[HTTP listener] The status code of the response from the load balancer.
backend_status_code	[HTTP listener] The status code of the response from the registered instance.
received_bytes	The size of the request, in bytes, received from the client (requester). [HTTP listener] The value includes the request body but not the headers. [TCP listener] The value includes the request body and the headers.
sent_bytes	The size of the response, in bytes, sent to the client (requester). [HTTP listener] The value includes the response body but not the headers. [TCP listener] The value includes the request body and the headers.
request	The request line from the client enclosed in double quotes and logged in the following format: HTTP Method + Protocol://Host header:port + Path + HTTP version. [TCP listener] The URL is three dashes, each separated by a space, and ending with a space ("- - - ").
user_agent	[HTTP/HTTPS listener] A User-Agent string that identifies the client that originated the request. The string consists of one or more product identifiers, product[/version]. If the string is longer than 8 KB, it is truncated.
ssl_cipher	[HTTPS/SSL listener] The SSL cipher. This value is recorded only if the incoming SSL/TLS connection was established after a successful negotiation. Otherwise, the value is set to -.
ssl_protocol	[HTTPS/SSL listener] The SSL protocol. This value is recorded only if the incoming SSL/TLS connection was established after a successful negotiation. Otherwise, the value is set to -.

Examples

Example HTTP Entry
The following is an example log entry for an HTTP listener (port 80 to port 80):

```
1 2015-05-13T23:39:43.945958Z my-loadbalancer 192.168.131.39:2817 10.0.0.1:80 0.000073 0.001048
      0.000057 200 200 0 29 "GET http://www.example.com:80/ HTTP/1.1" "curl/7.38.0" - -
```

Example HTTPS Entry
The following is an example log entry for an HTTPS listener (port 443 to port 80):

```
1 2015-05-13T23:39:43.945958Z my-loadbalancer 192.168.131.39:2817 10.0.0.1:80 0.000086 0.001048
      0.001337 200 200 0 57 "GET https://www.example.com:443/ HTTP/1.1" "curl/7.38.0" DHE-RSA-
      AES128-SHA TLSv1.2
```

Example TCP Entry

The following is an example log entry for an TCP listener (port 8080 to port 80):

```
1 2015-05-13T23:39:43.945958Z my-loadbalancer 192.168.131.39:2817 10.0.0.1:80 0.001069 0.000028
     0.000041 - - 82 305 "- - - " "-" - -
```

Example SSL Entry

The following is an example log entry for an SSL listener (port 8443 to port 80):

```
1 2015-05-13T23:39:43.945958Z my-loadbalancer 192.168.131.39:2817 10.0.0.1:80 0.001065 0.000015
     0.000023 - - 57 502 "- - - " "-" ECDHE-ECDSA-AES128-GCM-SHA256 TLSv1.2
```

Processing Access Logs

If there is a lot of demand on your website, your load balancer can generate log files with gigabytes of data. You might not be able to process such a large amount of data using line-by-line processing. Therefore, you might have to use analytical tools that provide parallel processing solutions. For example, you can use the following analytical tools to analyze and process access logs:

- Amazon Athena is an interactive query service that makes it easy to analyze data in Amazon S3 using standard SQL. For more information, see Querying Classic Load Balancer Logs in the *Amazon Athena User Guide*.
- Loggly
- Splunk
- Sumo Logic

Enable Access Logs for Your Classic Load Balancer

To enable access logs for your load balancer, you must specify the name of the Amazon S3 bucket where the load balancer will store the logs. You must also attach a bucket policy to this bucket that grants Elastic Load Balancing permission to write to the bucket.

Important
The bucket and your load balancer must be in the same region. The bucket can be owned by a different account than the account that owns the load balancer.

Topics

- Step 1: Create an S3 Bucket
- Step 2: Attach a Policy to Your S3 Bucket
- Step 3: Enable Access Logs
- Step 4: Verify that the Load Balancer Created a Test File in the S3 Bucket

Step 1: Create an S3 Bucket

You can create an S3 bucket using the Amazon S3 console. If you already have a bucket and want to use it to store the access logs, skip this step and go to Step 2: Attach a Policy to Your S3 Bucket to grant Elastic Load Balancing permission to write logs to your bucket.

Tip
If you will use the console to enable access logs, you can skip this step and have Elastic Load Balancing create a bucket with the required permissions for you. If you will use the AWS CLI to enable access logs, you must create the bucket and grant the required permissions yourself.

To create an Amazon S3 bucket

1. Open the Amazon S3 console at https://console.aws.amazon.com/s3/.

2. Choose **Create Bucket**.

3. On the **Create a Bucket** page, do the following:

    1. For **Bucket Name**, type a name for your bucket (for example, `my-loadbalancer-logs`). This name must be unique across all existing bucket names in Amazon S3. In some regions, there might be additional restrictions on bucket names. For more information, see Bucket Restrictions and Limitations in the *Amazon Simple Storage Service Developer Guide*.

    2. For **Region**, select the region where you created your load balancer.

    3. Choose **Create**.

Step 2: Attach a Policy to Your S3 Bucket

After you've created or identified your S3 bucket, you must attach a policy to the bucket. Bucket policies are a collection of JSON statements written in the access policy language to define access permissions for your bucket. Each statement includes information about a single permission and contains a series of elements.

If your bucket already has an attached policy, you can add the statements for the Elastic Load Balancing access log to the policy. If you do so, we recommend that you evaluate the resulting set of permissions to ensure that they are appropriate for the users that need access to the bucket for access logs.

Tip
If you will use the console to enable access logs, you can skip this step and have Elastic Load Balancing create a bucket with the required permissions for you.

114

To attach a policy statement to your bucket

1. Open the Amazon S3 console at https://console.aws.amazon.com/s3/.

2. Select the bucket, and then choose **Permissions**.

3. Choose **Bucket Policy**. If your bucket already has an attached policy, you can add the required statement to the existing policy.

4. Choose **Policy generator**. On the **AWS Policy Generator** page, do the following:

    1. For **Select Type of Policy**, select **S3 Bucket Policy**.

    2. For **Effect**, select **Allow** to allow access to the S3 bucket.

    3. For **Principal**, type the account ID for Elastic Load Balancing to grant Elastic Load Balancing access to the S3 bucket. Use the account ID that corresponds to the region for your load balancer and bucket.
    [See the AWS documentation website for more details]

       * This region requires a separate account. For more information, see AWS GovCloud (US).

       ** This region requires a separate account. For more information, see China (Beijing).

    4. For **Actions**, select PutObject to allow Elastic Load Balancing to store objects in the S3 bucket.

    5. For **Amazon Resource Name (ARN)**, type the ARN of the S3 bucket in the following format:

    ```
    1 arn:aws:s3:::bucket/prefix/AWSLogs/aws-account-id/*
    ```

    You must specify the ID of the AWS account that owns the load balancer, and you should not include the hyphens. For example:

    ```
    1 arn:aws:s3:::my-loadbalancer-logs/my-app/AWSLogs/123456789012/*
    ```

    Note that if you are using us-gov-west-1 region, use arn:aws-us-gov: instead of arn:aws: in the ARN.

6. Choose **Add Statement**, **Generate Policy**. The policy document should be similar to the following:

```
1  {
2    "Id": "Policy1429136655940",
3    "Version": "2012-10-17",
4    "Statement": [
5      {
6        "Sid": "Stmt1429136633762",
7        "Action": [
8          "s3:PutObject"
9        ],
10       "Effect": "Allow",
11       "Resource": "arn:aws:s3:::my-loadbalancer-logs/my-app/AWSLogs/123456789012/*",
12       "Principal": {
13         "AWS": [
14           "797873946194"
15         ]
16       }
17     }
18   ]
19 }
```

7. If you are creating a new bucket policy, copy the entire policy document, and then choose **Close**.

   If you are editing an existing bucket policy, copy the new statement from the policy document (the text between the [and] of the `Statement` element), and then choose **Close**.

5. Go back to the Amazon S3 console and paste the policy into the text area as appropriate.

6. Choose **Save**.

Step 3: Enable Access Logs

You can enable access logs using the AWS Management Console or the AWS CLI. Note that when you enable access logs using the console, you can have Elastic Load Balancing create the bucket for you with necessary permissions for the load balancer to write to your bucket.

Use the following example to capture and deliver logs to your S3 bucket every 60 minutes (the default interval).

To enable access logs for your load balancer using the console

1. Open the Amazon EC2 console at https://console.aws.amazon.com/ec2/.

2. On the navigation pane, under **LOAD BALANCING**, choose **Load Balancers**.

3. Select your load balancer.

4. On the **Description** tab, choose **Configure Access Logs**.

5. On the **Configure Access Logs** page, do the following:

   1. Choose **Enable access logs**.

   2. Leave **Interval** as the default, `60 minutes`.

   3. For **S3 location**, type the name of your S3 bucket, including the prefix (for example, `my-loadbalancer-logs/my-app`). You can specify the name of an existing bucket or a name for a new bucket.

   4. (Optional) If the bucket does not exist, choose **Create this location for me**. You must specify a name that is unique across all existing bucket names in Amazon S3 and follows the DNS naming conventions. For more information, see Rules for Bucket Naming in the *Amazon Simple Storage Service Developer Guide*.

   5. Choose **Save**.

To enable access logs for your load balancer using the AWS CLI

First, create a .json file that enables Elastic Load Balancing to capture and deliver logs every 60 minutes to the S3 bucket that you created for the logs:

```
1  {
2    "AccessLog": {
3      "Enabled": true,
4      "S3BucketName": "my-loadbalancer-logs",
5      "EmitInterval": 60,
6      "S3BucketPrefix": "my-app"
7    }
8  }
```

To enable access logs, specify the .json file in the modify-load-balancer-attributes command as follows:

```
1  aws elb modify-load-balancer-attributes --load-balancer-name my-loadbalancer --load-balancer-
     attributes file://my-json-file.json
```

The following is an example response:

```
 1  {
 2      "LoadBalancerAttributes": {
 3          "AccessLog": {
 4              "Enabled": true,
 5              "EmitInterval": 60,
 6              "S3BucketName": "my-loadbalancer-logs",
 7              "S3BucketPrefix": "my-app"
 8          }
 9      },
10      "LoadBalancerName": "my-loadbalancer"
11  }
```

Step 4: Verify that the Load Balancer Created a Test File in the S3 Bucket

After the access log is enabled for your load balancer, Elastic Load Balancing validates the S3 bucket and creates a test file. You can use the S3 console to verify that the test file was created.

To verify that Elastic Load Balancing created a test file in your S3 bucket

1. Open the Amazon S3 console at https://console.aws.amazon.com/s3/.

2. Select your S3 bucket.

3. Navigate to the test log file. The path should be as follows:

```
 1  my-bucket/prefix/AWSLogs/123456789012/ELBAccessLogTestFile
```

To manage the S3 bucket for your access logs

After you enable access logging, be sure to disable access logging before you delete the bucket with your access logs. Otherwise, if there is a new bucket with the same name and the required bucket policy created in an AWS account that you don't own, Elastic Load Balancing could write the access logs for your load balancer to this new bucket.

Disable Access Logs for Your Classic Load Balancer

You can disable access logs for your load balancer at any time. After you disable access logging, your access logs remain in your Amazon S3 until you delete the them. For information about managing your S3 bucket, see Working with Buckets in the *Amazon Simple Storage Service Console User Guide*.

To disable access logging using the console

1. Open the Amazon EC2 console at https://console.aws.amazon.com/ec2/.

2. On the navigation pane, under **LOAD BALANCING**, choose **Load Balancers**.

3. Select your load balancer.

4. On the **Description** tab, choose **Configure Access Logs**.

5. On the **Configure Access Logs** page, clear **Enable access logs**.

6. Choose **Save**.

To disable access logging using the AWS CLI
Use the following modify-load-balancer-attributes command to disable access logging:

```
1 aws elb modify-load-balancer-attributes --load-balancer-name my-loadbalancer --load-balancer-
    attributes "{\"AccessLog\":{\"Enabled\":false}}"
```

The following is an example response:

```
1  {
2      "LoadBalancerName": "my-loadbalancer",
3      "LoadBalancerAttributes": {
4          "AccessLog": {
5              "S3BucketName": "my-loadbalancer-logs",
6              "EmitInterval": 60,
7              "Enabled": false,
8              "S3BucketPrefix": "my-app"
9          }
10     }
11 }
```

AWS CloudTrail Logging for Your Classic Load Balancer

Elastic Load Balancing is integrated with AWS CloudTrail, which captures APIs calls and delivers log files to an Amazon S3 bucket that you specify. There is no cost to use CloudTrail. However, the standard rates for Amazon S3 apply.

CloudTrail logs calls to the AWS APIs, including the Elastic Load Balancing API, whenever you use them directly or indirectly through the AWS Management Console. You can use the information collected by CloudTrail to determine what API call was made, what source IP address was used, who made the call, when it was made, and so on. You can use AWS CloudTrail to capture information about the calls to the Elastic Load Balancing API made by or on behalf of your AWS account. For the complete list of Elastic Load Balancing API actions, see the Elastic Load Balancing API Reference version 2012-06-01.

To monitor other actions for your load balancer, such as when a client makes a request to your load balancer, use access logs. For more information, see Access Logs for Your Classic Load Balancer.

Topics

- Enable CloudTrail Event Logging
- Elastic Load Balancing Event Information

Enable CloudTrail Event Logging

If you haven't done so already, use the following steps to enable CloudTrail event logging for your account.

To enable CloudTrail event logging

1. Open the CloudTrail console at https://console.aws.amazon.com/cloudtrail/.

2. Choose **Get Started Now**.

3. For **Trail name**, type a name for your trail.

4. Leave **Apply trail to all regions** as **Yes**.

5. Select an existing S3 bucket for your CloudTrail log files, or create a new one. To create a new bucket, specify a unique name in **S3 bucket**. To use an existing bucket, change **Create a new S3 bucket** to **No** and then select your bucket from **S3 bucket**.

6. Choose **Turn on**.

The log files are written to your S3 bucket in the following location:

```
1   my-bucket/AWSLogs/123456789012/CloudTrail/region/yyyy/mm/dd/
```

For more information, see the AWS CloudTrail User Guide.

Elastic Load Balancing Event Information

The log files from CloudTrail contain event information in JSON format. An event record represents a single AWS API call and includes information about the requested action, such as the user that requested the action, the date and the time of the request, the request parameters, and the response elements.

The log files include event records for all AWS API calls for your AWS account, not just Elastic Load Balancing API calls. However, you can read the log files and scan for calls to the Elastic Load Balancing API using the `eventSource` element with the value `elasticloadbalancing.amazonaws.com`. To view information about a specific ELB API, such as `CreateLoadBalancer`, scan for the API name in the `eventName` element.

The following example shows CloudTrail log records for a user who created a load balancer and then deleted it using the AWS CLI. The user is identified by the `userIdentity` element. The CLI is identified by the `userAgent` element. The requested API calls (CreateLoadBalancer and DeleteLoadBalancer) are identified by the `eventName` element for each record. For more information about the different elements and values in a CloudTrail log file, see CloudTrail Event Reference in the *AWS CloudTrail User Guide*.

```
 1  {
 2    "Records": [
 3    {
 4      "eventVersion": "1.03",
 5      "userIdentity": {
 6        "type": "IAMUser",
 7        "principalId": "AIDAJDPLRKLG7UEXAMPLE",
 8        "arn": "arn:aws:iam::123456789012:user/Alice",
 9        "accountId": "123456789012",
10        "accessKeyId": "AKIAIOSFODNN7EXAMPLE",
11        "userName": "Alice"
12      },
13      "eventTime": "2016-04-01T15:31:48Z",
14      "eventSource": "elasticloadbalancing.amazonaws.com",
15      "eventName": "CreateLoadBalancer",
16      "awsRegion": "us-west-2",
17      "sourceIPAddress": "198.51.100.1",
18      "userAgent": "aws-cli/1.10.10 Python/2.7.9 Windows/7 botocore/1.4.1",
19      "requestParameters": {
20        "subnets": ["subnet-12345678","subnet-76543210"],
21        "loadBalancerName": "my-load-balancer",
22        "listeners": [{
23          "protocol: "HTTP",
24          "loadBalancerPort": 80,
25          "instanceProtocol": "HTTP",
26          "instancePort": 80
27        }]
28      },
29      "responseElements": {
30        "dNSName": "my-loadbalancer-1234567890.elb.amazonaws.com"
31      },
32      "requestID": "b9960276-b9b2-11e3-8a13-f1ef1EXAMPLE",
33      "eventID": "6f4ab5bd-2daa-4d00-be14-d92efEXAMPLE",
34      "eventType": "AwsApiCall",
35      "apiVersion": "2012-06-01",
36      "recipientAccountId": "123456789012"
37    },
38    {
39      "eventVersion: "1.03",
40      "userIdentity": {
41        "type": "IAMUser",
42        "principalId": "AIDAJDPLRKLG7UEXAMPLE",
43        "arn": "arn:aws:iam::123456789012:user/Alice",
44        "accountId": "123456789012",
45        "accessKeyId": "AKIAIOSFODNN7EXAMPLE",
46        "userName": "Alice"
47      },
48      "eventTime": "2016-04-08T12:39:25Z",
49      "eventSource": "elasticloadbalancing.amazonaws.com",
50      "eventName": "DeleteLoadBalancer",
51      "awsRegion": "us-west-2",
```

```
52      "sourceIPAddress": "198.51.100.1",
53      "userAgent": "aws-cli/1.10.10 Python/2.7.9 Windows/7 botocore/1.4.1",
54      "requestParameters": {
55         "loadBalancerName": "my-load-balancer"
56      },
57      "responseElements": null,
58      "requestID": "f0f17bb6-b9ba-11e3-9b20-999fdEXAMPLE",
59      "eventID": "4f99f0e8-5cf8-4c30-b6da-3b69fEXAMPLE"
60      "eventType": "AwsApiCall",
61      "apiVersion": "2012-06-01",
62      "recipientAccountId": "123456789012"
63   },
64    . . .
65 ]}
```

You can also use one of the Amazon partner solutions that integrate with CloudTrail to read and analyze your CloudTrail log files. For more information, see the AWS partners page.

Troubleshoot Your Classic Load Balancer

The following tables list the troubleshooting resources that you'll find useful as you work with a Classic Load Balancer.

API Errors

Error
CertificateNotFound: undefined
OutofService: A Transient Error Occurred

HTTP Errors

Error
HTTP 400: BAD_REQUEST
HTTP 405: METHOD_NOT_ALLOWED
HTTP 408: Request Timeout
HTTP 502: Bad Gateway
HTTP 503: Service Unavailable
HTTP 504: Gateway Timeout

Response Code Metrics

Response Code Metric
HTTPCode_ELB_4XX
HTTPCode_ELB_5XX
HTTPCode_Backend_2XX
HTTPCode_Backend_3XX
HTTPCode_Backend_4XX
HTTPCode_Backend_5XX

Health Check Issues

Issue
Health check target page error
Connection to the instances has timed out
Public key authentication is failing
Instance is not receiving traffic from the load balancer
Ports on instance are not open
Instances in an Auto Scaling group are failing the ELB health check

Connectivity Issues

Issue
Clients cannot connect to the load balancer

Instance Registration Issues

Issue
Taking too long to register an EC2 instance
Unable to register an instance launched from a paid AMI

Troubleshoot a Classic Load Balancer: API Errors

The following are error messages returned by Elastic Load Balancing API, the potential causes, and the steps you can take to resolve the issues.

Topics

- CertificateNotFound: undefined
- OutofService: A Transient Error Occurred

CertificateNotFound: undefined

Cause 1: There is a delay in propagating the certificate to all regions when it is created using the AWS Management Console. When this delay occurs, the error message is shown in the last step in the process of creating the load balancer.

Solution 1: Wait approximately 15 minutes and then try again. If the problem persists, go to the AWS Support Center for assistance.

Cause 2: If you are using the AWS CLI or API directly, you can receive this error if you provide an Amazon Resource Name (ARN) for a certificate that does not exist.

Solution 2: Use the Identity and Access Management (IAM) action GetServerCertificate to get the certificate ARN and verify that you provided the correct value for the ARN.

OutofService: A Transient Error Occurred

Cause: There is a transient internal problem within the Elastic Load Balancing service or the underlying network. This temporary issue might also occur when Elastic Load Balancing queries the health of the load balancer and its registered instances.

Solution: Retry the API call. If the problem persists, go to the AWS Support Center for assistance.

Troubleshoot a Classic Load Balancer: HTTP Errors

The HTTP method (also called the *verb*) specifies the action to be performed on the resource receiving an HTTP request. The standard methods for HTTP requests are defined in RFC 2616, Method Definitions. The standard methods include GET, POST, PUT, HEAD, and OPTIONS. Some web applications require (and sometimes introduce) methods that are extensions of HTTP/1.1 methods. Common examples of HTTP extended methods include PATCH, REPORT, MKCOL, PROPFIND, MOVE, and LOCK. Elastic Load Balancing accepts all standard and non-standard HTTP methods.

HTTP requests and responses use header fields to send information about the HTTP messages. Header fields are colon-separated name-value pairs that are separated by a cariage return (CR) and a line feed (LF). A standard set of HTTP header fields is definied in RFC 2616, Message Headers. For more information, see HTTP Headers and Classic Load Balancers.

When a load balancer receives an HTTP request, it checks for malformed requests and for the length of the method. The total method length in an HTTP request to a load balancer must not exceed 127 characters. If the HTTP request passes both checks, the load balancer sends the request to the EC2 instance. If the method field in the request is malformed, the load balancer responds with an HTTP 400: BAD_REQUEST error. If the length of the method in the request exceeds 127 characters, the load balancer responds with an HTTP 405: METHOD_NOT_ALLOWED error.

The EC2 instance processes a valid request by implementing the method in the request and sending a response back to the client. Your instances must be configured to handle both supported and unsupported methods.

The following are error messages returned by your load balancer, the potential causes, and the steps you can take to resolve the issues.

Topics

- HTTP 400: BAD_REQUEST
- HTTP 405: METHOD_NOT_ALLOWED
- HTTP 408: Request Timeout
- HTTP 502: Bad Gateway
- HTTP 503: Service Unavailable
- HTTP 504: Gateway Timeout

HTTP 400: BAD_REQUEST

Description: Indicates that the client sent a bad request.

Cause: The client sent a malformed request that does not meet HTTP specifications. For example, a request can't have spaces in the URL.

Solution: Connect directly to your instance and capture the details of the client request. Review the headers and the URL for malformed requests. Verify that the request meets HTTP specifications.

HTTP 405: METHOD_NOT_ALLOWED

Description: Indicates that the method length is not valid.

Cause: The length of the method in the request header exceeds 127 characters.

Solution: Check the length of the method.

HTTP 408: Request Timeout

Description: Indicates that the client cancelled the request or failed to send a full request.

Cause 1: A network interruption or a bad request construction, such as partially formed headers; specified content size doesn't match the actual content size transmitted; and so on.

Solution 1: Inspect the code that is making the request and try sending it directly to your registered instances (or a development / test environment) where you have more control over inspecting the actual request.

Cause 2: Connection to the client is closed (load balancer could not send a response)

Solution 2: Verify that the client is not closing the connection before a response is sent by using a packet sniffer on the machine making the request.

HTTP 502: Bad Gateway

Description: Indicates that the load balancer was unable to parse the response sent from a registered instance.

Cause: Malformed response from the instance or potentially an issue with the load balancer.

Solution: Verify that the response being sent from the instance conforms to HTTP specifications. Go to the AWS Support Center for assistance.

HTTP 503: Service Unavailable

Description: Indicates that either the load balancer or the registered instances are causing the error.

Cause 1: Insufficient capacity in the load balancer to handle the request.

Solution 1: This should be a transient issue and should not last more than a few minutes. If it persists, go to the AWS Support Center for assistance.

Cause 2: No registered instances.

Solution 2: Register at least one instance in every Availability Zone that your load balancer is configured to respond in. Verify this by looking at the `HealthyHostCount` metrics in CloudWatch. If you can't ensure that an instance is registered in each Availability Zone, we recommend enabling cross-zone load balancing. For more information, see Configure Cross-Zone Load Balancing for Your Classic Load Balancer.

Cause 3: No healthy instances.

Solution 3: Ensure that you have healthy instances in every Availability Zone that your load balancer is configured to respond in. Verify this by looking at the `HealthyHostCount` in CloudWatch.

HTTP 504: Gateway Timeout

Description: Indicates that the load balancer closed a connection because a request did not complete within the idle timeout period.

Cause 1: The application takes longer to respond than the configured idle timeout.

Solution 1: Monitor the `HTTPCode_ELB_5XX` and `Latency` metrics. If there is an increase in these metrics, it could be due to the application not responding within the idle timeout period. For details about the requests that are timing out, enable access logs on the load balancer and review the 504 response codes in the logs that are generated by Elastic Load Balancing. If necessary, you can increase your capacity or increase the configured idle timeout so that lengthy operations (such as uploading a large file) can complete. For more information, see Configure the Idle Connection Timeout for Your Classic Load Balancer and How do I troubleshoot Elastic Load Balancing high latency.

Cause 2: Registered instances closing the connection to Elastic Load Balancing.

Solution 2: Enable keep-alive settings on your EC2 instances and make sure that the keep-alive timeout is greater than the idle timeout settings of your load balancer.

Troubleshoot a Classic Load Balancer: Response Code Metrics

Your load balancer sends metrics to Amazon CloudWatch for the HTTP response codes sent to clients, identifying the source of the errors as either the load balancer or the registered instances. You can use the metrics returned by CloudWatch for your load balancer to troubleshoot issues. For more information, see CloudWatch Metrics for Your Classic Load Balancer.

The following are response code metrics returned by CloudWatch for your load balancer, the potential causes, and the steps you can take to resolve the issues.

Topics

- HTTPCode_ELB_4XX
- HTTPCode_ELB_5XX
- HTTPCode_Backend_2XX
- HTTPCode_Backend_3XX
- HTTPCode_Backend_4XX
- HTTPCode_Backend_5XX

HTTPCode_ELB_4XX

Cause: A malformed or canceled request from the client.

Solutions

- See HTTP 400: BAD_REQUEST.
- See HTTP 405: METHOD_NOT_ALLOWED.
- See HTTP 408: Request Timeout.

HTTPCode_ELB_5XX

Cause: Either the load balancer or the registered instance is causing the error or the load balancer is unable to parse the response.

Solutions

- See HTTP 502: Bad Gateway.
- See HTTP 503: Service Unavailable.
- See HTTP 504: Gateway Timeout.

HTTPCode_Backend_2XX

Cause: A normal, successful response from the registered instances.

Solution: None.

HTTPCode_Backend_3XX

Cause: A redirect response sent from the registered instances.

Solution: View the access logs or the error logs on your instance to determine the cause. Send requests directly to the instance (bypassing the load balancer) to view the responses.

HTTPCode_Backend_4XX

Cause: A client error response sent from the registered instances.

Solution: View the access or error logs on your instances to determine the cause. Send requests directly to the instance (bypass the load balancer) to view the responses.

Note

If the client cancels an HTTP request that was initiated with a `Transfer-Encoding: chunked` header, there is a known issue where the load balancer forwards the request to the instance even though the client canceled the request. This can cause backend errors.

HTTPCode_Backend_5XX

Cause: A server error response sent from the registered instances.

Solution: View the access logs or the error logs on your instances to determine the cause. Send requests directly to the instance (bypass the load balancer) to view the responses.

Note

If the client cancels an HTTP request that was initiated with a `Transfer-Encoding: chunked` header, there is a known issue where the load balancer forwards the request to the instance even though the client canceled the request. This can cause backend errors.

Troubleshoot a Classic Load Balancer: Health Checks

Your load balancer checks the health of its registered instances using either the default health check configuration provided by Elastic Load Balancing or a custom health check configuration that you specify. The health check configuration contains information such as the protocol, ping port, ping path, response timeout, and health check interval. An instance is considered healthy if it returns a 200 response code within the health check interval. For more information, see Configure Health Checks for Your Classic Load Balancer.

If the current state of some or all your instances is `OutOfService` and the description field displays the message that the `Instance has failed at least the Unhealthy Threshold number of health checks consecutively`, the instances have failed the load balancer health check. The following are the issues to look for, the potential causes, and the steps you can take to resolve the issues.

Topics

- Health check target page error
- Connection to the instances has timed out
- Public key authentication is failing
- Instance is not receiving traffic from the load balancer
- Ports on instance are not open
- Instances in an Auto Scaling group are failing the ELB health check

Health check target page error

Problem: An HTTP GET request issued to the instance on the specified ping port and the ping path (for example, HTTP:80/index.html) receives a non-200 response code.

Cause 1: No target page is configured on the instance.

Solution 1: Create a target page (for example, `index.html`) on each registered instance and specify its path as the ping path.

Cause 2: The value of the Content-Length header in the response is not set.

Solution 2: If the response includes a body, then either set the Content-Length header to a value greater than or equal to zero, or set the Transfer-Encoding value to 'chunked'.

Cause 3: The application is not configured to receive requests from the load balancer or to return a 200 response code.

Solution 3: Check the application on your instance to investigate the cause.

Connection to the instances has timed out

Problem: Health check requests from your load balancer to your EC2 instances are timing out or failing intermittently.

First, verify the issue by connecting directly with the instance. We recommend that you connect to your instance from within the network using the private IP address of the instance.

Use the following command for a TCP connection:

```
1 telnet private-IP-address-of-the-instance port
```

Use the following command for an HTTP or HTTPS connection:

```
1 curl -I private-IP-address-of-the-instance:port/health-check-target-page
```

If you are using an HTTP/HTTPS connection and getting a non-200 response, see Health check target page error. If you are able to connect directly to the instance, check for the following:

Cause 1: The instance is failing to respond within the configured response timeout period.

Solution 1: Adjust the response timeout settings in your load balancer health check configuration.

Cause 2: The instance is under significant load and is taking longer than your configured response timeout period to respond.

Solution 2:

- Check the monitoring graph for over-utilization of CPU. For information, see Get Statistics for a Specific EC2 Instance in the *Amazon EC2 User Guide for Linux Instances*.
- Check the utilization of other application resources, such as memory or limits, by connecting to your EC2 instances.
- If necessary, add more instances or enable Auto Scaling. For more information, see the Amazon EC2 Auto Scaling User Guide.

Cause 3: If you are using an HTTP or an HTTPS connection and the health check is being performed on a target page specified in the ping path field (for example, `HTTP:80/index.html`), the target page might be taking longer to respond than your configured timeout.

Solution 3: Use a simpler health check target page or adjust the health check interval settings.

Public key authentication is failing

Problem: A load balancer configured to use the HTTPS or SSL protocol with back-end authentication enabled fails public key authentication.

Cause: The public key on the SSL certificate does not match the public key configured on the load balancer. Use the `s_client` command to see the list of server certificates in the certificate chain. For more information, see s_client in the OpenSSL documentation.

Solution: Your might need to update your SSL certificate. If your SSL certificate is current, try re-installing it on your load balancer. For more information, see Replace the SSL Certificate for Your Classic Load Balancer.

Instance is not receiving traffic from the load balancer

Problem: The security group for the instance is blocking the traffic from the load balancer.

Do a packet capture on the instance to verify the issue. Use the following command:

```
1 # tcpdump port health-check-port
```

Cause 1: The security group associated with the instance does not allow traffic from the load balancer.

Solution 1: Edit the instance security group to allow traffic from the load balancer. Add a rule to allow all traffic from the load balancer security group.

Cause 2: The security group of your load balancer in a VPC does not allow traffic to the EC2 instances.

Solution 2: Edit the security group of your load balancer to allow traffic to the subnets and the EC2 instances.

For information about managing security groups for EC2-Classic, see Security Groups for Instances in EC2-Classic.

For information about managing security groups for a VPC, see Security Groups for Load Balancers in a VPC.

131

Ports on instance are not open

Problem: The health check sent to the EC2 instance by the load balancer is blocked by the port or a firewall.

Verify the issue by using the following command:

```
1 netstat -ant
```

Cause: The specified health port or the listener port (if configured differently) is not open. Both the port specified for the health check and the listener port must be open and listening.

Solution: Open up the listener port and the port specified in your health check configuration (if configured differently) on your instances to receive load balancer traffic.

Instances in an Auto Scaling group are failing the ELB health check

Problem: Instances in your Auto Scaling group pass the default Auto Scaling health check but fail the ELB health check.

Cause: Auto Scaling uses EC2 status checks to detect hardware and software issues with the instances, but the load balancer performs health checks by sending a request to the instance and waiting for a 200 response code, or by establishing a TCP connection (for a TCP-based health check) with the instance.

An instance might fail the ELB health check because an application running on the instance has issues that cause the load balancer to consider the instance out of service. This instance might pass the Auto Scaling health check; it would not be replaced by the Auto Scaling policy because it is considered healthy based on the EC2 status check.

Solution: Use the ELB health check for your Auto Scaling group. When you use the ELB health check, Auto Scaling determines the health status of your instances by checking the results of both the instance status check and the ELB health check. For more information, see Adding Health Checks to your Auto Scaling Group in the *Amazon EC2 Auto Scaling User Guide*.

Troubleshoot a Classic Load Balancer: Client Connectivity

If your Internet-facing load balancer in a VPC is not responding to requests, check for the following:

Your Internet-facing load balancer is attached to a private subnet
Verify that you specified public subnets for your load balancer. A public subnet has a route to the Internet Gateway for your virtual private cloud (VPC).

A security group or network ACL does not allow traffic
The security group for the load balancer and any network ACLs for the load balancer subnets must allow inbound traffic from the clients and outbound traffic to the clients on the listener ports. For more information, see Security Groups for Load Balancers in a VPC.

Troubleshoot a Classic Load Balancer: Instance Registration

When you register an instance with your load balancer, there are a number of steps that are taken before the load balancer can begin to send requests to your instance.

The following are issues your load balancer might encounter when registering your EC2 instances, the potential causes, and the steps you can take to resolve the issues.

Topics

- Taking too long to register an EC2 instance
- Unable to register an instance launched from a paid AMI

Taking too long to register an EC2 instance

Problem: Registered EC2 instances are taking longer than expected to be in the `InService` state.

Cause: Your instance might be failing the health check. After the initial instance registration steps are completed (it can take up to approximately 30 seconds), the load balancer starts sending health check requests. Your instance is not `InService` until one health check succeeds.

Solution: See Connection to the instances has timed out.

Unable to register an instance launched from a paid AMI

Problem: Elastic Load Balancing is not registering an instance launched using a paid AMI.

Cause: Your instances might have been launched using a paid AMI from Amazon DevPay.

Solution: Elastic Load Balancing does not support registering instances launched using paid AMIs from Amazon DevPay. Note that you can use paid AMIs from AWS Marketplace. If you are already using a paid AMI from AWS Marketplace and are unable to register an instance launched from that paid AMI, go to the AWS Support Center for assistance.

Limits for Your Classic Load Balancer

To view the current limits for your Classic Load Balancers, use the **Limits** page of the Amazon EC2 console or the describe-account-limits (AWS CLI) command. To request a limit increase, use the Elastic Load Balancing Limits form.

Your AWS account has the following limits related to Classic Load Balancers.

- Load balancers per region: 20 *
- Listeners per load balancer: 100
- Security groups per load balancer: 5
- Subnets per Availability Zone per load balancer: 1

* This limit includes both your Application Load Balancers and your Classic Load Balancers.

Document History

The following table describes the Elastic Load Balancing releases and important changes for Classic Load Balancers.

Feature	Description	Release Date
Classic Load Balancers	With the introduction of the new Application Load Balancers, load balancers created with the 2016-06-01 API are now known as *Classic Load Balancers*. For more information about the differences between these types of load balancers, see What is Elastic Load Balancing? in the *Elastic Load Balancing User Guide*.	August 11, 2016
Support for AWS Certificate Manager (ACM)	You can request an SSL/TLS certificate from ACM and deploy it to your load balancer. For more information, see SSL/TLS Certificates for Classic Load Balancers.	January 21, 2016
Support for additional ports	Load balancers in a VPC can listen on any port in the range 1-65535. For more information, see Listeners for Your Classic Load Balancer.	September 15, 2015
Additional fields for access log entries	Added the `user_agent`, `ssl_cipher`, and `ssl_protocol` fields. For more information, see Access Log Files.	May 18, 2015
Support for registering linked EC2-Classic instances	Added support for registering linked EC2-Classic instances with your load balancer.	January 19, 2015

Feature	Description	Release Date
Support for tagging your load balancer	You can use tags to organize and manage your load balancers. Starting with this release, Elastic Load Balancing CLI (ELB CLI) has been replaced by AWS Command Line Interface (AWS CLI), a unified tool to manage multiple AWS services. New features released after ELB CLI version 1.0.35.0 (dated 7/24/14) will be included in the AWS CLI only. If you are currently using the ELB CLI, we recommend that you start using the AWS Command Line Interface (AWS CLI) instead. For more information, see the AWS Command Line Interface User Guide.	August 11, 2014
idle connection timeout	You can configure the idle connection timeout for your load balancer.	July 24, 2014
Support for granting IAM users and groups access to specific load balancers or API actions	You can create an IAM policy to grant IAM users and groups access to specific load balancers or API actions.	May 12, 2014
Support for AWS CloudTrail	You can use CloudTrail to capture API calls made by or on behalf of your AWS account using the ELB API, the AWS Management Console, the ELB CLI, or the AWS CLI. For more information, see AWS CloudTrail Logging for Your Classic Load Balancer.	April 04, 2014
connection draining	Added information about connection draining. With this support you can enable your load balancer to stop sending new requests to the registered instance when the instance is de-registering or when the instance becomes unhealthy, while keeping the existing connections open. For more information, see Configure Connection Draining for Your Classic Load Balancer.	March 20, 2014

Feature	Description	Release Date
access logs	You can enable your load balancer to capture detailed information about the requests sent to your load balancer and store it in an S3 bucket. For more information, see Access Logs for Your Classic Load Balancer.	March 06, 2014
Support for TLSv1.1-1.2	Added information about TLSv1.1-1.2 protocol support for load balancers configured with HTTPS/SSL listeners. With this support, Elastic Load Balancing also updates the predefined SSL negotiation configurations. For information about the updated predefined SSL negotiation configurations, see SSL Negotiation Configurations for Classic Load Balancers. For information about updating your current SSL negotiation configuration, see Update the SSL Negotiation Configuration of Your Classic Load Balancer.	February 19, 2014
cross-zone load balancing	Added information about enabling cross-zone load balancing for your load balancer. For more information, see Configure Cross-Zone Load Balancing for Your Classic Load Balancer	November 06, 2013
Additional CloudWatch Metrics	Added information about the additional Cloudwatch metrics reported by Elastic Load Balancing. For more information, see CloudWatch Metrics for Your Classic Load Balancer.	October 28, 2013
Support for Proxy Protocol	Added information about Proxy Protocol support for load balancers configured for TCP/SSL connections. For more information, see Proxy Protocol Header.	July 30, 2013
Support for DNS failover	Added information about configuring Route 53 DNS failover for load balancers. For more information, see Configure DNS Failover for Your Load Balancer.	June 03, 2013

Feature	Description	Release Date
Console support for viewing CloudWatch metrics and creating alarms	Added information about viewing CloudWatch metrics and creating alarms for a specified load balancer using the console. For more information, see CloudWatch Metrics for Your Classic Load Balancer.	March 28, 2013
Support for registering EC2 instances in a default VPC	Added support for EC2 instances launched in a default VPC.	March 11, 2013
internal load balancers	With this release, a load balancer in a virtual private cloud (VPC) can be made either internal or Internet-facing. An internal load balancer has a publicly resolvable DNS name that resolves to private IP addresses. An Internet-facing load balancer has a publicly resolvable DNS name that resolves to public IP addresses. For more information, see Create an Internal Classic Load Balancer.	June 10, 2012
Console support for managing listeners, cipher settings, and SSL certificates	For information, see Configure an HTTPS Listener for Your Classic Load Balancer and Replace the SSL Certificate for Your Classic Load Balancer.	May 18, 2012
Support for Elastic Load Balancing in Amazon VPC	Added support for creating a load balancer in a virtual private cloud (VPC).	November 21, 2011
Amazon CloudWatch	You can monitor your load balancer using CloudWatch. For more information, see CloudWatch Metrics for Your Classic Load Balancer.	October 17, 2011
Additional security features	You can configure SSL ciphers, back-end SSL, and back-end server authentication. For more information, see Create a Classic Load Balancer with an HTTPS Listener.	August 30, 2011
zone apex domain name	For more information, see Configure a Custom Domain Name for Your Classic Load Balancer.	May 24, 2011

Feature	Description	Release Date
instance lock-down	You can use the security group provided by Elastic Load Balancing to lock down your back-end instance. For more information, see Security Groups for Instances in EC2-Classic.	May 24, 2011
Support for IPv6	You can use Internet Protocol version 6 (IPv6) with your load balancer in EC2-Classic.	May 24, 2011
Support for X-Forwarded-Proto and X-Forwarded-Port headers	The X-Forwarded-Proto header indicates the protocol of the originating request, and the X-Forwarded-Port header indicates the port of the originating request. The addition of these headers to requests enables customers to determine if an incoming request to their load balancer is encrypted, and the specific port on the load balancer that the request was received on. For more information, see HTTP Headers and Classic Load Balancers.	October 27, 2010
Support for HTTPS	With this release, you can leverage the SSL/TLS protocol for encrypting traffic and offload SSL processing from the application instance to the load balancer. This feature also provides centralized management of SSL server certificates at the load balancer, rather than managing certificates on individual application instances.	October 14, 2010
Support for AWS Identity and Access Management (IAM)	Added support for IAM.	September 02, 2010
sticky sessions	For more information, see Configure Sticky Sessions for Your Classic Load Balancer.	April 07, 2010
AWS SDK for Java	Added support for the SDK for Java.	March 22, 2010
AWS SDK for .NET	Added support for the AWS SDK for .NET.	November 11, 2009
New service	Initial public beta release of Elastic Load Balancing.	May 18, 2009